A marketing dashboard can be your catalyst for success and credibility. But where do you start? What do you include? And how will you ensure that your marketing dashboard will add to marketing's accountability?

Marketing by the Dashboard Light: How to Get More Insight, Foresight, and Accountability from Your Marketing Investments gives you insight into planning, design, construction, and implementation of an effective marketing dashboard. And for those who already have one, *Marketing by the Dashboard Light* gives you the information you need to help retool and focus your dashboard for maximum effect.

More Praise for *Marketing by the Dashboard Light*

"This is the best practical guide to the dashboard and the marketing metrics that should appear on it. Every business person concerned with their sources of cash flow should read it several times."

Tim Ambler, Senior Fellow, London Business School, and author of *Marketing and the Bottom Line*

"Accountability is finally here. Tracking and measuring marketing and communication is finally possible and Pat tells you how."

Don E. Schultz, Professor Emeritus, Northwestern University, and author of *IMC: The Next Generation*

"I really enjoyed reading *Marketing by the Dashboard Light*. Its content is very useful and will certainly enable me to better assist our clients. Thank you for such a wonderful tool."

Greg Timpany, Director of Research, Wilkin Guge Marketing

Marketing by the Dashboard Light

How to Get More Insight, Foresight, and Accountability from Your Marketing Investments

By Patrick LaPointe

ISBN 0-9787211-2-8

www.MarketingNPV.com

Published in cooperation with the Association of National Advertisers.

To all the hundreds of people from whom I've stolen ideas and drawn inspiration over the years. I only hope you find this a valuable means of getting even with me.

Table of Contents

Part I
Planning the Marketing Dashboard: Setting Up for Success

Part III

Going Live: Implementing Your Dashboard

Acknowledgments

The first thing I need to acknowledge is that this book is a work in progress. It will never be finished.

Much like our broader exploration of measuring marketing effectiveness, the real learning is just beginning. True, we've been helped along (as the concepts here were) by some of the most brilliant minds in marketing today, including Don Schultz of Northwestern, Tim Ambler of the London Business School, Gary Lilien of Penn State, and Dave Reibstein of Wharton. Each has patiently shared his invaluable perspective and tools and tolerated the endless stream of "but if that's true then why …" questions. More than 15 years out of grad school and I'm getting a second chance to work with this incredible faculty. It doesn't get any better than this.

We were also very fortunate to have had the opportunity to interview dozens of CMOs to help us understand what is working (and not working) in marketing measurement today. A few who generously offered their insights and experiences include John Costello (formerly CMO of The Home Depot), Becky Saeger of Charles Schwab, Jim Garrity of Wachovia, Joe Tripodi of Allstate, Larry Light of McDonald's, Anne MacDonald of Citigroup, Mike Winkler (formerly CMO of HP), Scott Deaver of Avis, Scott Fuson of Dow Corning, Arun Sinha of Pitney Bowes, and many others who shared their thoughts informally but contributed to our framework significantly. Thank you all.

And there were more than a few subject-area experts whose impact can easily be seen in the final product. First among equals in this category is Jonathan Knowles, brand strategist extraordinaire (and a

U.S. government-certified "alien of exceptional ability") whose creative and articulate views on brand measurement helped form the pillars of our brand scorecard strategy. Thanks to David Haigh for his thoughtful insight on brand valuation. Jim Lenskold gets credit for not only pushing the thinking behind marketing ROI techniques and process, but also for coming up with the title of this book. Jim Donius also deserves a note of thanks for testing our views on the integration of research and analytics, as Rick Watrall does for continually updating our understanding of integrated modeling in marketing decision processes. And finally, thanks to Beth Weesner of Marketing Transformations for help in refining our thinking about MRM technologies and their role in dashboard development.

I say "we" because I've had a tremendous amount of help in writing this book from friends and co-workers. Tina Anagnostis worked tirelessly to edit and re-edit both text and graphics. Lisa Holton contributed hundreds of hours as a valuable Contributing Editor. Nicole Shillingford kept the other wolves at bay so I could steal precious hours to think and write. Ruth Stevens tightened our thinking and writing. Noushin Nourizadeh made it all look great. And Jennifer Zipf meticulously managed the final editing, layout, and production to perfection despite my many failures to remain on schedule.

I would also like to thank the ANA, especially Barbara Bacci Mirque, for believing that the end product would be good despite long periods of silence on our progress.

And finally, I owe a tremendous debt of gratitude to my family for all the days and nights they allowed me to hide away in my office and write. Please don't ever let me do it again.

Introduction

"**I** feel pretty good about all the measurement activity we have going on around here. We've got some incredibly bright people doing some very sophisticated things to determine the effect of our marketing investments. But I still don't feel we have developed any synthesis across those various ad-hoc efforts. We've got some great models, but they're not linked well to our equally great research. We're getting better — but we're not getting to a bigger picture, just getting better at drilling down into the smaller ones."

In the course of interviewing dozens of *Fortune* 100 chief marketing officers (CMOs) for this book, we heard that comment (or a close approximation of it) time and again. So often, in fact, that it would be unfair for us to attribute it to any single CMO, but rather to a majority of the group.

The early stages of marketing effectiveness measurement (and let's face it, we are still in the early days) have been characterized by great progress in quantifying the quantifiable. As an industry, we have made some terrific strides in measuring those things for which data is available. We've learned to build mix models to optimize media expenditures. We've reallocated resources across channels and products. And we've gone a long way in many industries to understanding customer-specific profitability and the ROI of individual marketing initiatives.

Yet as the quote above shows, there is still a hunger for answers to the BIG questions about marketing. Not the one that asks, "What is our ROI on that campaign?" (although that's important), but the one that answers the CEO question of, "Should I double my marketing investment or cut it in half?" Without the ability to view effectiveness *horizontally* — across programs, initiatives, campaigns, segments, geographies — we are relegated to optimizing the current world view instead of creating new ones.

The reason we seem to be stuck in ad-hoc "measuredom" is that most of us have heretofore approached marketing measurement from a tools-and-data perspective instead of an organizational business-process view. The process of designing and implementing a *marketing dashboard* as described herein is intended to address exactly that error in perspective.

The creation of a marketing dashboard forces alignment between company goals and marketing objectives. Executed properly, it is a big step in giving your executive committee the financial and strategic transparency they've been demanding. Better measurement and better communication will give your department the freedom — and hopefully, the funding — to do more of what you do best.

The best marketing dashboards hone our instincts and intuition. They move talented people away from their dependence on past-performance data and change the orientation to look ahead to the horizon. They can be leading indicators to tell you when marketing initiatives are working, and quick-correction systems when they're not. In short, the dashboard delivers better marketing accountability, which translates into higher credibility.

It's all in how you build it.

A well-executed dashboard can make marketing effectiveness transparent to the CEO and the entire executive committee of your firm so they never again need to ask the question, "We gave you $5 million for XYZ project. What exactly did we get for that money?"

The process of designing and deploying a dashboard provides the discipline of what to measure and then conveys the performance on those metrics. In fact, done correctly, the focus of an effective marketing dashboard is more on where the next $5 million should go, not where the last $5 million went.

There is no "industry standard" marketing dashboard. There shouldn't be. Dashboarding is an evolving practice, especially in marketing. In a few years, the best of the best will emerge to tell their stories at conferences around the world. But until then (and likely even after), the best dashboard in the industry is the one that best serves *your* organization.

A marketing dashboard needs to be a customized, relevant, context-specific tool that fits the learning style and unique business dynamics of your organization — from financial reporting requirements to data availability to channel structures to sales funnel processes.

A well-executed dashboard takes a thorough look at your marketing team — the strength of your staff, the data and metrics you depend on now, your alliances with other departments, and an honest assessment of how you communicate. As you'll see, the dashboard is merely the visual display of the machine's inner workings. You and your people are the machine.

This book is about building feedback mechanisms to gain more control of your marketing impact. It's about forming a solid foundation for learning that over time will enlighten the CMO and his or her team to get better at predicting and anticipating the potential impact of marketing programs, initiatives, strategies, or changes to the marketing portfolio.

Analytical methodologies will always be important to this process, and sound science can help to focus and magnify the effect of marketing creativity and instinct. But you create real value for shareholders and improve your influence among other constituencies when the analytics are implemented in the context of good organizational practices — structure, process, skills, and tools.

The right marketing dashboard puts the most insightful dials and digits in front of you in a package that's simple, informative, and illuminating — all at a single glance. It needs to be dynamic, and it needs to reflect how your marketing organization is working at any point in time, not six months ago or even two weeks ago.

That's why there really is no "one size fits all" available for this purpose. You design a dashboard to fit your need for understanding and insight — period. And while many software companies offer all sorts of prepackaged solutions, the best solution is *always* the one that communicates most effectively the things that are most important to you. And that particular solution may come in the most modest, homegrown package.

Start Your Engines

Here's where your thinking should start. A marketing dashboard is an evolutionary journey. It starts best with a small set of key metrics and a limited number of drill-down page views. Initially, it may appear as a single page view that gets updated weekly and passed around in hard copy. Eventually, it can grow to become a real-time window into dozens of key metrics that update every second on your intranet. But right from the very start, it must be inviting, easy to use, and a solid fit with your learning culture.

Last but not least, your dashboard must tell you the most valuable information *right now*, not what you needed to know last week, last month, or last year.

And that's going to require some innovation.

But once you've finished with this book, you'll be armed with the necessary framework to design, build, and implement your marketing dashboard — resulting in more insight, foresight, and accountability for *and* from your marketing investments.

The most common question we get about the marketing dashboard is, "What do we measure?"

Read on. We're going to help you figure that out.

PART I

Planning the Marketing Dashboard: Setting Up for Success

What Is a Marketing Dashboard?
The New Way to Capture, Shape,
and Improve Marketing
Effectiveness and Efficiency

The dashboard of a car, a plane, even a video game gives you a lot of crucial information. How fast are you going? How far have you traveled? How much fuel do you have left? How hot is the engine?

A marketing dashboard provides you with the same up-to-the-minute information necessary to run your operation — sales vs. forecast, distribution channel effectiveness, brand equity evolution, human capital development — whatever is relevant to the role of marketing in your organization. An effective dashboard might focus on only three critical metrics or show the top 20. It could appear in your inbox monthly in the form of a nice color printout or be beamed over the company intranet first thing each morning.

The most useful marketing dashboard allows you to measure and manage your marketing effectiveness in ways you probably haven't tried. It will verify all the things that are working well. It will also shine a bright light on systems, projects, staff, and processes with the opportunity to improve. It will change the way you gather information while helping you to simplify the complex world of moving measurement targets. Most of all, an effective dashboard will focus your thinking and significantly improve the way you communicate it to others.

And yes, it just might reveal for all to see where the marketing investments are paying off and where they aren't. That's the tough part.

From what we see in many organizations, marketing — unlike IT, sales, or manufacturing — isn't always given the same credit by top management for having a direct impact on the organization's bottom line. Certainly, marketing creates ideas and initiatives that drive growth. Though most CEOs would agree that marketing plays a role in the company's success, they just don't know how to quantify that role. This is what makes it so difficult to get incremental funding for marketing programs or even to defend existing funding when dollars get tight.

This is something a marketing dashboard can help change.

Many of today's marketing organizations have made significant strides in the development of sophisticated analytical approaches to improve marketing measurement. Ph.D. statisticians are now common in most large marketing departments, as are research departments, media-mix models, and models for assessing the return from a proposed initiative.

But what are they really measuring?

Figure 1.1 shows the three most common measurement "pathways" marketers are pursuing today.

FIGURE 1.1 — COMMON MEASUREMENT PATHWAYS

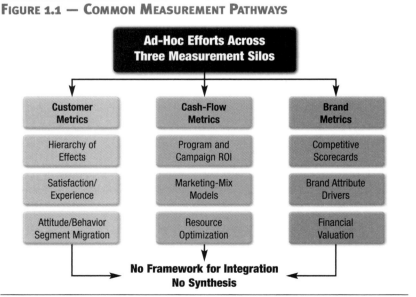

Source: Adapted from a model by Don E. Schultz, Ph.D. Reprinted with permission. Copyright © 2005 Agora, Inc.

The customer metrics pathway looks at how prospects become customers. From awareness to preference to trial to repeat purchase, many companies track progression through a "hierarchy of effects" model to track evolution of broad market potential to specific revenue opportunities. This customer pathway also tends to include robust attitudinal data on customer segments — why they want what they want or buy what they buy — which is often correlated with actual customer transactional data to create a robust segmentation model. The segments are then monitored for "mobility" — the directional progression of prospects/customers from one segment to a presumably more valuable one. In many B2B organizations, this customer pathway can go all the way to developing a customer-specific P&L.

The cash-flow metrics pathway focuses on efficiency of marketing expenditures in achieving short-term returns. Program and campaign ROI models measure the immediate impact or net present value of profits expected to be derived from a given investment initiative. Media-mix models use statistical regression techniques to identify which combinations of media placements, integrated media elements, and even copy executions generate the most profitable response from customers. And all of those inputs feed a focus on optimizing resource allocation in the context of generating near-term results.

The brand metrics pathway seeks to track the development of the longer-term impact of marketing through brand health. Survey-based tracking studies gauge customer and prospective customer perspectives on the brand — its functionality, personality, accessibility, and value propositions. Brand scorecards track the evolution of these perspectives over time within market segments and across multiple constituencies like employees, regulators, and community influencers. And many have taken the successful leap to develop financial models for estimating the financial value of the brand as a means of determining the aggregation of assets on the balance sheet as an outcome of marketing investments.

While most larger marketing departments have managed to build effective measurement systems within one or more of the three pathways, few have been able to synthesize across pathways in a manner that helps one pathway explain another or clarifies the predictive drivers of the business on a broader level.

For most companies, it's actually not possible to do this scientifically because it's not an econometric modeling problem solvable by equations and computers. Each pathway measures very different components of marketing effectiveness in very different ways. Some are shorter term and some longer term. Linking them algorithmically forces you to make some very large assumptions that may be unreliable in the face of actual marketplace dynamics. And even if you *can* solve it algorithmically, you will likely have to employ statistical techniques of such sophistication that no one in either marketing or finance will understand sufficiently to embrace and defend the method.

A marketing dashboard helps present the insights from all three of the pathways in a graphically related view that facilitates the human brain's incredible power to find subtle contextual links. This is the point where the "art" and "science" of marketing need to blend.

Most CMOs still struggle to close the gap and embrace the scientific measurement practices and the remaining "art" components that seemingly defy measurement in any reasonable fashion yet are highly correlated with success. As with most other aspects of business, the science enables greatness, but the application of imagination and innovation is what delivers it.

It is this very "art" component of marketing that requires the CMO to have the full confidence and trust of his or her CEO and the executive committee. To win this credibility, today's CMO needs to find ways of measuring risk that are transparent and understandable to all. If you want top management to accept the art you bring to the process, you have to do a better job of quantifying the chances for success. Only in the rarest organizations will marketing chiefs get by with the words "trust me." These days, leaps of faith come with pretty heavy price tags.

But credibility is a hard-won attribute that comes at the end of a long history of earned respect. As shown in figure 1.2, credibility:

- starts with demonstrated alignment with the rest of the organization on goals and objectives;
- builds with the implementation of an overall measurement framework based on as much scientific rigor as appropriate;

- expands through demonstrated objectivity and transparency of reporting results; and

- cements itself in a high degree of personal accountability.

FIGURE 1.2 — THE PATH TO CREDIBILITY

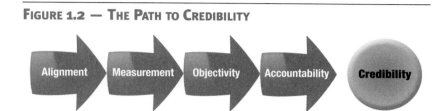

A marketing dashboard is an easy-to-understand way to illustrate to the rest of the organization your alignment, measurement orientation, objectivity, transparency, and ultimate accountability. In short, it puts credibility into a tangible, visible form.

How "Marketing" Has Outgrown the Marketing Department

A marketing plan is a clever device intended to arrest the intelligence of the chief financial officer just long enough to get the budget approved.

— Tim Ambler misquoting humorist Stephen Leacock[1]

In early 2004, the Association of National Advertisers (ANA) and consulting firm Booz Allen Hamilton undertook a study to examine the relevance of marketing, marketing departments, and CMOs (whether they operate under that title or another) in today's business climate.[2] Among the findings:

- More than 75% of marketers and non-marketers said that marketing has become more important to their companies during the past five years. But at more than half of all companies, marketing and the CEO agenda were reported to be misaligned.

- Higher expectations for marketing have driven nearly 70% of all companies to reorganize their marketing departments during the 12 months prior to the survey. Yet a major component of many such reorganizations — the position of chief marketing officer — remains ill-defined.

■ Measurable outcomes are now expected for marketing programs — 66% of executives say true ROI analytics are marketing's greatest need. But most companies are still using "intermediary" metrics — such as awareness — instead of working toward strong links to financial value.

The pressure on companies to find new sources of topline growth has placed a renewed emphasis on "marketing." Such traditional marketing-centric activities as creating new products or services, finding new markets, and maintaining and growing existing customer relationships are increasingly being shared across the organization in customer service, operations, manufacturing, and elsewhere. It's arguable that the company's marketing needs have outgrown the marketing department.

At the same time, the general business climate is demanding robust measurement and financial controls in all areas of the organization. In most organizations, this has shifted considerable decision-influencing power to finance. For marketing executives, this has been quite a wake-up call.

FIGURE 1.3 — REASONS FOR PRESSURE ON MARKETING

Source: ANA & Booz Allen Hamilton Study of Marketing Organizations 2004, ANA/Booz Allen Analysis. Reprinted with permission.

The problem is compounded by the fact that freshly trained marketing recruits from business schools get little if any preparation for the challenges they're most likely to face today.

One of the biggest problems with marketing today is found in the business schools, where finance majors spend the vast majority of their time in courses dealing primarily with manufacturing organizations — i.e., management of tangible assets. Few get exposed to the intangible value created in services or B2B, which is where you see the greatest need for alignment between marketing and finance today. Thus, MBAs can manage a factory but not a group of customers or a set of intellectual properties. And, they have no clue about how to deal with critical issues where finance and marketing come face to face.

— Don E. Schultz, founder of the Integrated Marketing Communications graduate program at Northwestern University and author of *IMC: The Next Generation*[3]

As competing divisions within the firm get more proficient in measuring their own initiatives and performance, they're seeking greater accountability and support from marketing. In many cases, division heads think, perhaps rightly, that they know the marketing function better than the marketers do.

That front-office conflict may be the smoldering fire sending you one or more of the following smoke signals:

- Nobody credits marketing with any specific impact on the bottom line.
- The budget cycle is a tension-filled fight to keep last year's spending levels intact and protect programs and headcount.
- Your CFO isn't buying your marketing-mix model or any efforts to link brand equities to profits.

Data-driven measurement of marketing is nothing new. Since the evolution of the marketing function in the 1940s and '50s, companies have always attempted to gauge the effectiveness of their marketing expenditures. In those days, the modest technology of the times and the near absence of rapid media cost escalation or academic involvement led marketing executives to focus mostly on "intermediary" measures like awareness, preference, and other "researchable" variables.

Today, the Internet and the 24-hour information cycle have transformed the way buyers get information. Yet marketing measurement methods haven't adapted to accommodate these realities that have utterly changed the ways we do business.

Today, for better or worse, we face three driving forces:

■ fast-changing technology that allows us to capture, warehouse, and analyze previously unimaginable amounts of data in near real time;

■ rapid cost escalation in media and message distribution that requires us to re-educate ourselves and sharpen our expenditure patterns ruthlessly; and

■ the broadening number of brilliant academics who are now focusing exclusively on the marketing discipline — even if they are driven by their own competitive need to get published, they are advancing mathematical science in marketing in some extremely innovative ways.

Do you feel you're in the loop with all of these developments? If not, you're not alone.

Marketing is dancing as fast as it can, but it's clearly not fast enough. Opportunities to gather data may be improving through technology and information-sharing, but the underlying skills and business processes of your people are probably not keeping pace.

How do you know if you're in trouble? Consider the following:

■ Factions within your own marketing department are fighting for budget dollars and attention in a battle of politics and power. Note that these are people you *thought* should be working together.

■ You have dozens or possibly hundreds of projects going, but no idea which ones are making the greatest financial contribution to your company's bottom line.

■ No one can say for sure — least of all you — what the impact would be if certain key initiatives were dropped completely.

These are big challenges we're talking about. But by working to build alignment, instill measurement discipline, demonstrate objectivity and transparency, and promote accountability, the marketing dashboard might help you put these problems in turnaround. It is most certainly *not* a panacea to all (or even most) marketing ills. But in today's increasingly complex organizations, a return to focus, simple process discipline, and attention to only the most important goals should be paramount.

Today, we find ourselves at an inflection point in marketing measurement. For the first time, we really are in a position to measure what we should, not just what we can. That leaves us with a lot of choices. To make the right ones, marketers need a structure that allows them to learn and evolve quickly and efficiently.

What a Marketing Dashboard Does

There are five key benefits to employing a marketing dashboard:

1. A marketing dashboard aligns marketing objectives to the company's financial objectives and corporate strategy through the selection of critical metrics and sharing of results.

2. The marketing dashboard not only creates organizational alignment *within* marketing by linking all expenditures back to a smaller set of focused objectives, it clarifies the relationships *between* marketing and other corporate functional areas. It crystallizes roles and responsibilities to ensure everyone understands the interdependencies between departments or functions. The result of all this alignment makes it easy to see, if not directly measure, greater job satisfaction in a culture of performance and success.

3. The marketing dashboard establishes direct links between spending and profits. It uses graphical representations of crucial metrics in ways that begin to show, often for the first time, the causal relationships between marketing initiatives and financial results. It portrays historical data in a fashion that makes it easier for any corporate brain to grasp and understand the implications. The result? A better ability to make smart resource

allocations and increase both the efficiency and effectiveness of marketing spending.

4. It creates a learning organization that makes decisions on hard facts supplemented with experiential intuition, rather than battles of intuition punctuated by a few dangerous facts. The real benefit of this evolution is a dramatic reduction in time spent in highly politicized arguments. That speeds decision making.

5. It creates transparency in marketing's goals, operations, and performance, creating stronger alliances outside the department. This elevates marketing's perceived accountability to earn the trust and confidence of the CEO, the CFO, the board, and other key decision makers throughout the company.

Regardless of how sophisticated you are at measuring your current marketing efforts, the dashboard can make you better. It's a very accommodating tool. It benefits from, but does not require, a high degree of sophistication of analytics. It doesn't require that there be a robust IT infrastructure. It doesn't require any special skill set at all — other than the ability to determine what's important to measure.

The Basic Construction

Like all things worthwhile, creating a marketing dashboard is a fairly detailed undertaking with the potential for lots of moving parts. It will take three to six months to define the dashboard, identify its stages of evolution, map and secure the necessary data flows, test its design on the user community for feedback, and instill a sense of ownership.

Of course, you can always implement something fast and cheap quite quickly, but the purpose of the dashboard is to inform the key decision makers on the current and potential state of the business and help them make better choices. So as the old IT saying goes, "Garbage in, garbage out."

Every dashboard should be as unique as the organization it serves. Whatever physical form it takes, the dashboard's objective is to report succinctly and clearly on the progress marketing is making toward its defined business objectives. For a retailing chain, for instance, a dashboard might track how marketing is helping an aggressive store expansion plan meet the company's profitability target while monitoring how well brand and reputation assets are laying the groundwork for new private label products. For a chemical manufacturer, the dashboard might focus on customer profitability segments and the velocity of movement through the sales funnel.

An effective dashboard is alive. It adapts and changes with the organization as objectives are clarified and redefined, as causal relationships are established between metrics, and as confidence in predictive measures grows. In short, about the only thing you know for certain about your first version of a marketing dashboard is that it will likely look very different a year or two down the road. And that is as it should be.

There are two primary goals of any dashboard: diagnostic insight and predictive foresight — with a special emphasis on the latter. Some dashboard metrics are diagnostic, looking at what has happened and trying to discern why. The most important ones you'll come to rely on are predictive, using the diagnostic experience to forecast future results under various assumptions of circumstances and resource allocations.

FIGURE 1.4 — THE MARKETING DASHBOARD

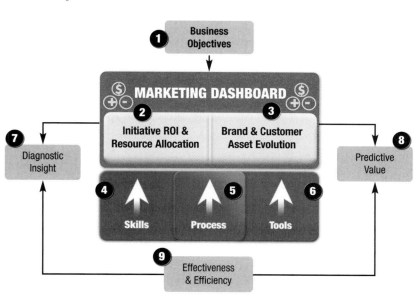

The marketing dashboard — in virtually any form — builds a way for you and all the people above and below you on the organizational chart to see what's working, as quickly as possible, forming a solid foundation for learning. Figure 1.4 shows the path to developing the dashboard.

A marketing dashboard is made up of the following parts:

1. **Business objectives:** Your starting point. These are the goals of the company, translated into a set of marketing objectives. All ideas and initiatives should be filtered through this prism.

2. **Initiative ROI and resource allocation:** An important part of the dashboard is measuring the incremental cash flows generated by marketing programs and initiatives in the near term. In addition, the dashboard is an excellent tool to measure the efficiency of resource allocation in dollars, headcount, or both.

3. **Brand and customer asset evolution:** At least equal in importance to the short-term results is the longer-term evolution of the corporate assets entrusted to marketing — most often including the brand and the customer perceptions/relationships. The dashboard can provide a read of how the assets have been growing and how they are likely to progress.

4. **Skills:** A well-rounded dashboard tracks the skills and competencies of the marketing team against a clear set of proficiency goals.

5. **Process:** The dashboard also provides insight into the execution of critical business processes required to deliver on the desired customer value propositions.

6. **Tools:** Less a metric than an enabler, successful dashboarding employs and continuously refines tools to increase insight and reduce effort in both producing and distributing it.

7. **Diagnostic insight:** The dashboard must push beyond portrayal of *what* is happening to *why* it is happening, providing insight into where prior expectations were inaccurate to help hone the process of setting expectations and forecasts for the future.

8. **Predictive value:** The difference between a helpful dashboard and a truly effective one is the degree to which it uses the diagnostic insight and predicts what is *likely* to happen on critical performance dimensions absent intervention.

9. **Effectiveness and efficiency:** The end goal — enhancing both the efficiency and the effectiveness of marketing investments,

thereby improving the ROI and the NPV (net present value) for the firm.

A Few Important Considerations

One of the key traps for dashboard builders is a tendency to overlook the dynamic nature of their macro environment and focus too much on the "within the walls" corporate issues. That's like building a measuring device for what you already know. Dashboards that reflect the "outside-in" perspective are much more likely to be insightful than those limited to the "inside-out" perspective. Identifying and closely monitoring external factors likely to cause significant changes to the business is what makes a dashboard dynamic. Building an addiction to this type of information in your organization is critical.

Another trap is the tendency to fill the dashboard with too many "intermediary metrics" — those that tell marketers something about program effectiveness, but stop short of linking that effect to financial or strategic results. The easy choices often involve brand awareness, trial, and customer or prospect preferences and intentions. Absent some mechanism to translate these intermediaries into financial or strategic value, they are best left to the drill-down pages of the dashboard, which we'll discuss in greater detail later. If you lead with what you can most easily measure, you're just going to reinforce for top management that your nifty little device is nothing more than a more graphical way of "spinning" the same old marketing mumbo jumbo.

Finally, dashboard effectiveness should be defined in terms of the degree to which it is embraced throughout the organization and adopted into the decision making of the key influencers of company strategy and resource allocation. In other words, you want the percentage of senior executives who both believe and understand what the dashboard is presenting to be very, very high.

While you can be successful with a dashboard solely targeted to the marketing staff, its real value lies in your ability to share it with all the marketing stakeholders that exist outside your department. You definitely want to sell it to your CEO and CFO, but there are probably other executives in the company who may think they know your job better than you. Include them in the mix and impress them with your ability to lead the discussion.

CMO VIEW: STARTING THE PROCESS

Rebecca Saeger
EXECUTIVE VICE PRESIDENT, CHIEF MARKETING OFFICER
The Charles Schwab Corporation

I've been here through a period of great change. We've changed CEOs — Charles Schwab has come back to run our company — and we've all gone through a real cost-leadership exercise. So, the microscope has definitely been on marketing.

I do think that there has been a strong belief here that marketing, particularly direct marketing, drives the business. But at the same time I found that we have more data than we could possibly use. So, if someone were to ask a question like, "How is such-and-such working?" five people would come out of the woodwork, each with a different answer from a different perspective.

We had programs that were measured based on response rates based on advertising. We had programs that would be measured based on a predetermined ROI goal. We had programs that weren't being measured at all. It was really kind of all over the place. I think that part of it is that we are in an industry that's been evolving at the speed of light over the last few years. My focus has been on trying to get some sense of alignment from business objectives down through marketing execution, really getting people to understand the thread that ties those things together.

And we have developed some tools — not a dashboard per se, but a marketing planning tool that accounts for every marketing program we have. We plug in objectives, costs, NPV projections and what spits out the back end is how we are doing based on where we are in the life of that project. This way, we can say what worked, what didn't, what paid out, and what is on schedule to pay out. Our system is evolving, but it's grounded in analysis of where we will make the most money. If the profitability proposition isn't there, it doesn't get marketing dollars. We have a corporate target for marketing spend and juggle it through the planning process to see who gets what based on corporate objectives. It's portfolio management, really.

We are in the process of developing a dashboard right now, with an emphasis on using it as a management tool and not just an ad hoc reporting structure. Our first objective is to make it a diagnostic tool that gets everyone looking at the same numbers at the same time. We're not going to build some multimillion-dollar online dashboard; we're just trying to wrestle the data into manageable sets of metrics.

Part of our process is involving our business-leader partners in helping identify the right things to measure. We have a retail marketing and sales council that meets biweekly. It consists of the executive who runs the retail business, the one who runs the sales channel, the one who runs the customer segment business units, myself, and our CEO. We are in the process of developing the dashboards that we need to look at every couple of weeks so we can tell if we really got our money's worth on what we spent on marketing.

To a large degree, it's a question of accountability and trust building, not just at the CEO level, but with my peers across the organization. Once you have established that accountability where people know that you're clearly focused on the same things as they are and you're making every effort to measure the effectiveness of your allocation of the resources, they're a lot more open to how you can contribute to help their part of the business.

I've known several senior marketers who were not as willing to be open with the rest of the business and not very trusting people. But when I look around the table with the management team, nobody there wants to see anyone fail because we are all in this together. Once they trust that you are listening to them and aligned with what they're trying to do, they are more open to hearing your point of view about your own area of responsibility. So, when I say to them, "Guys, this is what we need to do with the advertising" or "This is what we need to do with this customer segment," they are more likely to take our recommendation. That's not to say that I can just walk in and ask for $20 million because I want it. But if I have a good case, it gets consideration at a level where they're not doubting that the $20 million would do what I say that it would, but only deciding whether that's the place where the company really needs to spend $20 million right now.

Where will we be in a year? I think we are going to have a really aligned management team within the firm and within our marketing organization too. Top management will be consistently looking at the same metrics around the business and I am excited because I think we are going to be looking at the brand as a business tool much more aggressively.[4]

CONCLUSION

Creating a marketing dashboard is neither fast nor easy. It requires taking a hard look at your organization, your processes, and the often-harsh perceptions others in your organization have of what you're doing. The payoff comes when you create a predictive system of measurement that's easy to understand, revolutionizes your operation, and creates credibility with senior staff.

The marketing dashboard is also a way to refresh or blow up the measurement systems you've been using for years. The drive to create a simple, at-a-glance picture of how your marketing initiatives are creating value for your organization will shine a light on all your processes and results. It's a risky move, but one worth taking.

SOURCES

1. Ambler, Tim, Senior Fellow, London Business School.

2. ANA (Association of National Advertisers) and Booz Allen Hamilton, "Are CMOs Irrelevant? Organization, Value, Accountability, and the New Marketing Agenda," 2004.

3. Schultz, Don E., Professor Emeritus, Northwestern University; President, Agora, Inc.

4. Saeger, Rebecca, The Charles Schwab Corporation.

See the Road Ahead ...
Where Are You on the Ladder of Insight?

O ne of the best things about a marketing dashboard is that the very process of building one can help establish greater financial and measurement discipline in your organization. It can give a marketing department with little or no infrastructure a way to start and a moderately sophisticated one a path to evolve with a way to pinpoint problems and hidden successes as never before.

Think of it this way: In training to become a pilot, you first learn to fly a single-engine propeller plane in clear skies so you can see everything around you. Eventually, you graduate to multiple engines and flying "by instrument," which allows you to fly at night and in low visibility.

The instruments are intended to keep you oriented and level when your instincts might otherwise mislead. Any pilot will tell you that learning to trust the instruments is a difficult thing to do at first, but once you do, you find yourself free to enjoy the flexibility and feedback they offer. You stay on course more often and get where you're going faster and more efficiently.

Running a marketing department these days is increasingly like learning to fly on instruments. There are so many data points to consider, so many potential obstacles, so many other marketing messages crowding the airwaves and mailboxes, and, of course, so many "false horizons." By necessity, most marketing professionals have had to evolve toward the use of carefully designed instruments to keep on course when the sheer speed of business begins to outpace their instincts.

So what are these instruments and just how are marketers using them to their advantage? The answer depends on the nature of your industry, your company goals, and the level of sophistication you're starting from. While a single book isn't a great place to dive deep into specifics relative to any single industry or company culture, it can be helpful in describing the spectrum of sophistication that exists across companies.

In this chapter, we're going to examine the evolutionary process of marketing departments in their quest for knowledge about the return on every marketing dollar spent. To do so, we use a framework called the "Ladder of Insight," sort of a Darwinian evolutionary chart of where marketing organizations often find themselves on the road to better measurement. Understanding where your company is on the ladder helps you see the starting point for your dashboard, as well as the road ahead. In other words, it gives you a clearer context for the direction you want your dashboard to take you in.

Climbing the Ladder of Insight

We use a ladder as a metaphor to suggest that as you climb higher, you get better visibility and perspective. It also seems appropriate to think that people in the organization will increasingly look up to you and welcome your leadership as you climb higher.

There are five distinct levels on this ladder:

FIGURE 2.1 — THE LADDER OF INSIGHT

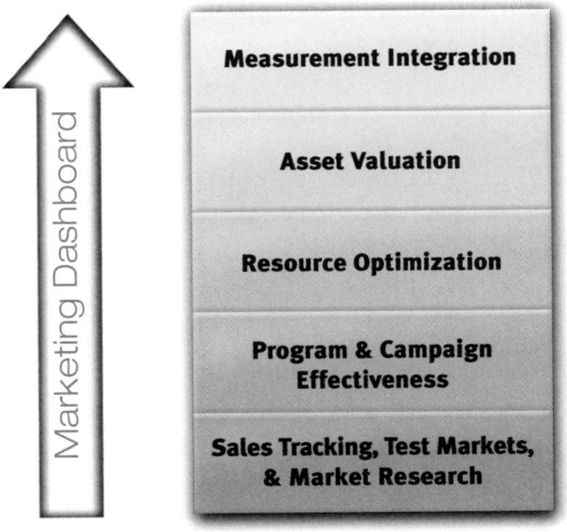

Marketing Dashboard

Measurement Integration

Asset Valuation

Resource Optimization

Program & Campaign Effectiveness

Sales Tracking, Test Markets, & Market Research

Level 1 — Sales Tracking, Test Markets, and Market Research

This is the baseline level. Marketing results are tabulated by product/market/region/channel and reported at least monthly.[1] More often, they might be reported weekly or daily and occasionally in real time. The only correlations between marketing activities and business results are measured by the incremental reported sales in selected test markets vs. matched control markets. In fact, many are still not using matched control markets, but relying on the dangerous practice of looking at pre-/post-measures in the same geography, which are risky due to the inability to accurately read the effect of the marketing stimulus from the rest of the potential variables.

At this first level, market research is used to regularly measure customer and prospect awareness, brand perceptions, purchase intentions, and maybe even share of market.

Level 2 — Program and Campaign Effectiveness

At this level, the CMO requires that select new programs and initiatives are presented with an expected return based upon their anticipated incremental profit contribution (after accounting for fully loaded costs).

This forecast return is compared to alternative opportunities the company has at the time, and the decision to commit or abandon is made based upon allocating budget dollars to achieve the best outcome. While in progress, these initiatives are regularly reassessed at each point that another round of discretionary expenditures are required. When they have run their course, the programs are subjected to a final measurement and studied post-mortem for learnings and insights into future opportunities for improvement. Note that at this level and the next, programs and initiatives intended solely to enhance the customer and prospect perception of the company or brand (e.g., brand advertising, sponsorships, community relations) are often excluded from the analysis. Why? Because their impact is difficult to quantify in terms of dollars, and their contributions generally accrue over an extended period of time.

Going from Level 1 to Level 2

If you got these basics down, you can reach further by taking the following steps:

- Begin to assemble sales and margin data in an accessible format with frequent refreshment. You might want to ask IT to help assemble a "data mart" that you can access directly and use to export data into desktop applications like Excel.

- Set up job-cost accounting so expenditures can be tracked back to specific initiatives.

- Work with finance to adopt a flexible modeling approach to measure the effectiveness and efficiency of campaigns and initiatives built on agreed definitions of gross margin, contribution margin, pre-tax profit, and net income. Also agree on rates for cost of capital and target ROI hurdles. Secure their help in developing these analyses — finance should see these metrics and agree on the methodology long before it's time to pass judgment on them.

- Begin requiring that all new programs, campaigns, or initiatives with expected completion timeframes of six months or less submit an ROI analysis to get funding approvals. Then match each initiative's forecast with a post-analysis reflecting actual results. Use gaps and differentials as the basis for model refinement and calibration, and continue training of individuals and the team as a whole.

- After the first six-month cycle, institute quarterly assessments of projects midstream and introduce interim assessment methods to re-examine the project commitment against possible changes in the investment opportunity horizon.

- Resist the temptation to reward highest ROI initiatives in favor of rewarding managers visibly for support of and adherence to the forecasting system. That way you keep the emphasis on applying the process correctly, not just on getting the highest ROI score — a pursuit that could encourage managers to win by not spending as opposed to spending wisely.

- You might consider installing campaign management software to help standardize tracking and reporting. This is particularly helpful if you are running dozens of concurrent marketing campaign initiatives or customer promotions.

- Begin correlating market research data on awareness, brand equities, purchase intentions, etc., to financial results like sales and gross margins. Chart the factors together on the same graph and look for patterns over a period of time. Manually overlay significant events you're aware of, such as competitive activity, regulatory activity, macroeconomic and geopolitical events, etc., on the same chart to help discover any possible relationships between the events and the results.

Level 3 — Optimizing Resource Allocation

Once the discipline of financial assessment is adopted across most individual marketing initiatives, the entire "portfolio" of possible initiatives competes for scarce budget dollars on the basis of forecast returns. This comparison may be performed monthly or quarterly to allow resources to be reallocated as market opportunities and threats change. Optimization techniques are used to solve for the highest possible return in terms of media mix, segment emphasis, and channel management.

At this level, highly evolved marketing leaders will take the additional step of requiring that all initiatives be presented with a risk-adjusted forecast so their true potential can be better assessed. Inflating or "padding" the expected risk-adjusted return of any given initiative becomes difficult, perhaps impossible, since flawed assumptions are likely to be uncovered in the very first progress review, if they aren't during the initial risk assessment.

GOING FROM LEVEL 2 TO LEVEL 3

If you're already confidently operating at Level 2, here are a few steps to help you progress further:

- Continue to invest in your data mart, making it more comprehensive and accessible. Consider adding an analytics package to help standardize access to data and ensure that comparisons between programs and initiatives are done on an apples-to-apples basis.

- As you increase the percentage of total marketing spending subject to the financial analysis process, work with accounting to devise a reasonable method of overhead allocation to each project or initiative. Involve team leaders in defining overhead and establish rules for which projects get an allocation and which don't.

- Introduce and train the team on the use of risk assessment tools to become part of each project-funding request. Require that all forecast returns be risk-adjusted and make larger projects subject to peer review to accelerate standardization of the risk assessment process.

- Apply optimization techniques to allocate limited funds between programs, customer segments, channels, acquisition vs. retention, media mix, or other areas where "necessities" or "opportunities" exceed available resources in the near term.

- Begin to measure and monitor correlations of interdependence between various marketing activities to ascertain which programs are complementary and which elements of multifaceted initiatives are most directly related to the results.

- Refine and test correlations among branding initiatives, strategic factors from earlier stages, and financial results to improve predictive/explanatory relationships.

Level 4 — Asset Valuation

At Level 4, the department is comfortable with its ability to measure short-term incremental cash flows generated by marketing initiatives. Now it turns its attention to the more challenging questions of measuring the financial return on expenditures principally designed to enhance brand assets (company/brand awareness, appeal, and preference) or customer assets (customer value, customer lifetime value, or customer franchise value). This is where the relationship between CMOs and CEOs could get dicey.

The challenge here is that many such efforts in this category are only intended to increase the *likelihood* that a customer or prospect will purchase or repurchase from the company again, not to specifically "ask for an order." Also, most corporate or branding initiatives are part of integrated programs that stimulate particular purchase activity, so it's tough to come up with an overall success measurement for a branding program.

Marketers at Level 4 are making the effort to identify the measurable outcomes of such activities over time (i.e., awareness, brand preference, pricing power, etc.) and correlate those intermediary measures with expected financial benefits in both the near and long term. Most continuously track these key metrics and use statistical techniques to monitor their correlation with sales, gross margins, profits, and "goodwill" that contributes to the company's value as a whole.

It's important to recognize that companies operating at Level 4 didn't develop these skills overnight. They achieved this level of success through a consistent approach that led to reliable correlations between market metrics and financial value. Further, the exact formula used is less relevant than the fact that one was agreed to by marketing, the CEO, and the CFO, and that any evolution of it has been done with careful attention to maintaining historic reliability.

KEY QUESTIONS THAT INEVITABLY ARISE AT LEVEL 4

Q: What good is a consistent measurement methodology in an increasingly discontinuous world where competitors enter and exit the market freely, and technology reinvents communication and distribution channels annually?

A: The benefit is not so much the measurement algorithms themselves, but having a methodology to use as the basis for comparing and a process to guide the consideration of applying, adapting, or replacing it. This will minimize the risks of reacting on instinct to changes that might appear to be more or less threatening than they really are. A dashboard serves much the same purpose, by encouraging the long view and putting specific market-altering events in context. It helps improve the quality of perspective when decisions need to be made.

Q: Is it fruitless to try to prove with financial analysis the benefit of long-term brand-building activities?
A. No, it's fruitless to resist. If you can't do it, the company will eventually bring in someone who can. Besides, the question is rarely a referendum on brand building. More often, it is raised in contemplation of cutting or increasing the budget for it. Without a sound measurement methodology to help forecast the implications of those scenarios, the answer will usually be to cut.

Q: Is the question of long-term brand-building effectiveness related to the quality of creative advertising?
A. Clearly. But how many times can we blame a lack of results on "bad creative" before we either admit that brand advertising has too high a risk factor or change the way we go about developing advertising?

GOING FROM LEVEL 3 TO LEVEL 4

Having laid the groundwork in Levels 1 through 3, correlations must be made at this point between pure branding or "corporate marketing" initiatives and financial results:

- Engage research, planning, and finance teams to work together to explore the correlations between branding expenditures to increases in profitability, even though they might be on a time-delayed basis.

- Charter — or shadow — the same teams to evaluate changes in the market value of the company relative to comparable benchmarks to see if there is a correlation to branding activities.

- Absent any clear determinations in either case above, your CMO, CEO, and CFO must discuss the strategic benefits of continuing branding or corporate activities and decide if they should be held to a stand-alone measurement standard, allocated against other marketing activities, or continued for "qualitative" reasons. Regardless, the agreed methodology ultimately forms the basis for the brand scorecard section of your marketing dashboard (see Chapter 6).

But be forewarned. An agreement to a "qualitative" rationale for continued branding activities almost always leads to subsequent budget battles over intuition-driven assessments of ad copy. Informal agreements within the executive team can be quickly forgotten with the first market tightening or change at the executive level.

Level 5 — Measurement Integration

Here, at the top of the ladder, all marketing activities are planned and measured in an integrated framework that takes into account both short- and long-term return.

To accomplish this, companies take an approach that weighs financial efficiency and productivity measures like ROI and NPV against strategic effectiveness metrics like market share, customer retention, satisfaction, employee satisfaction, and others.

Others adopt a more financially driven model such as Economic Value Added (EVA®), in which the cumulative effect of marketing for the period in question is measured by determining after-tax incremental profits from marketing expenditures (aggregated from Level 2, 3, and 4 activities and modifying certain assumptions about expenses vs. depreciable assets). The result is then found by subtracting the benchmark rate of return on the capital deployed.

A few major multinationals like Diageo and Unilever have gone so far as to integrate their far-flung operations into a common measurement structure that allows corporate resource allocation not only by product category, but also by market.

Regardless of the differences in measurement methodologies, the common traits of companies who have reached this highest level include:

- goals and objectives are set (and periodically revisited) using very specific, quantifiable metrics;

- measurement has been integrated into the planning process upfront and is employed through each activity's lifecycle, not just at the end;

- all expenditures are evaluated in the context of maximizing the overall outcome since management compensation (at the VP level and above) is tied to delivery at or above goals;

- the measurement is done at all levels by all marketing managers and integrated into their daily responsibilities, not assigned to a dedicated analysis group of "measurement police"; and

- measurement is structured with the business focus to meet the needs of the CEO, the CFO, and possibly the entire executive committee.

GOING FROM LEVEL 4 TO LEVEL 5

The path beyond Level 4 is largely dependent upon the degree to which a company can confidently measure the benefit of its branding and corporate activities in financial terms. Companies that cannot make that link, yet choose to continue the branding, can consider more of a "balanced scorecard" approach to building a dashboard that integrates hard (e.g., financial) and soft (e.g., awareness and perceptual) measures. Other important considerations include:

- Focusing on just a few top-level objectives, making sure that all are quantified in terms of what is to be achieved, the magnitude of achievement desired, and deadlines (e.g., increase brand preference scores by 15% within 12 months).

- Align all marketing activities with one of these few scorecard elements so relationships can be clearly defined and measured.

- Design compensation and recognition programs for marketing team leaders to reinforce their relationships to specific scorecard elements and also the balance of team goals.

Companies that *can* quantify the financial benefit of branding or corporate marketing activities can apply the same assessment methodology or metric for all marketing expenditures:

- Translate the expected return from brand or corporate marketing initiatives into these common metrics.

- Allocate and reallocate resources regularly, optimizing the desired balance of short- and long-term results.
- Link management compensation directly to incremental improvements in the selected metric(s).
- Integrate marketing expenditure requests back into the corporate resource allocation process using the same metrics as IT, HR, or manufacturing.

Questions You Should Ask

So now that you have a sense of where your organization stands on the Ladder of Insight and how to climb higher, ask yourself a few final questions to guide the ascent.

1. **What are your true objectives?** How will the marketing department and the company as a whole benefit from this evolution? Can you quantify this benefit to help gauge the potential return on the investment you will make in achieving it? If even a broad-based cost/return effort evades you, you might need some outside help to avoid false steps that have big costs in terms of credibility.

2. **How broad is the commitment to improvement?** Is this an effort championed by marketing with active support of its CEO and CFO? Or is it another challenge thrust upon you by top management that you'll try to respond to so you can get back to your real work? Unless the CMO, CFO, and CEO are enthusiastically supportive of an agreed set of objectives along with a process and timeline, there will be disputes over methodology, parochial resource defense, and mixed messages sent to the troops. And the troops have to do the heavy lifting.

3. **Speaking of the troops ... how are their skills?** Do you have the change-leaders within your current marketing organization to help you succeed? Can they drive toward higher levels of achievement?

The answers will help you frame a more realistic plan for improvement and set clearer expectations both within and beyond the marketing department.

CASE STUDY

HILTON HOTELS — USING THE BALANCED SCORECARD AS A FOUNDATION FOR THE MARKETING DASHBOARD

Hilton Hotels Corp. adopted the balanced scorecard in 1997 and made it the foundation for translating its corporate strategic vision to marketing, brand management, and operations. That framework has allowed the hotelier to reach out to its hotel guests, company shareholders, and employees as never before.

It has also served as the starting point for a simple yet effective scorecard that tracks both hard and soft metrics to provide as complete a picture as possible.

Hilton has an annual business-planning process that links its business strategy with critical tactical actions. Each key performance indicator (KPI) on the scorecard is derived from and aligns with one of four value drivers. There are eight KPIs. Some are diagnostic lagging indicators that show the outcomes of a strategy employed. Others are more predictive lead indicators that help modify marketing execution to take advantage of future opportunities.

Each of the KPIs is reported as a numerical score, which is why this is more of a scorecard than a dashboard. However, the use of three color zones — green (shown in figure 2.2 in light blue) indicating performance at or beyond the goal, yellow (shown in gray) signaling results slightly below the goal, and red (shown in dark blue) flagging performance well below the goal — increase the graphic absorption potential, making it a much more effective structure overall.

By communicating results visually to show strengths and weaknesses, marketing can clearly see how it is performing on its objectives and where to focus its efforts, not to mention its resources. In this case, it is clear that Hilton needs to address both the widespread problems at Hotel E, as well as the overall poor scores on the mystery shopper program.

To assist in identifying areas of potential value growth, customized priority reports identify the key drivers of customer satisfaction upon which marketing and its colleagues in other departments should focus. This helps the organization concentrate its efforts on the elements of a Hilton stay most important to guests.

Hilton puts a priority on improving its strategies, business processes, and balanced scorecard toward ensuring that its stated value drivers adequately describe how the company can best meet its corporate goals. Continuous improvement of the Hilton balanced scorecard, nicknamed STP for Situation-Target-Proposal, is a multiphase process for determining a course of action.

FIGURE 2.2 — HILTON PERFORMANCE DASHBOARD

Rank	Rating	Property	Brand standards compliance	Operational effectiveness (EBITDA)	Revenue maximization		Value proposition			
					Room RevPAR*	RevPAR* index	Guest comment cards	Customer-satisfaction tracking study	Team-member survey	Mystery shopper
1	6	Hotel A	100%	$20.730	$123.77	123.7	6.36	6.20	60%	94.91%
2	6	Hotel B	100%	8.065	$73.15	106.4	6.35	6.09	75%	91.32%
3	5	Hotel C	100%	2.584	101.12	103.8	6.30	6.04	81%	89.84%
37	3	Hotel D	95%	16.252	93.59	99.9	5.73	5.10	69%	85.31%
51	0	Hotel E	95%	3.055	68.17	94.0	6.08	5.68	67%	88.67%

Significantly short of goal (red zone)	Less than goal (yellow zone)	Meets or exceeds goal (green zone)

* Revenue Per Available Room

Although the power of the Hilton brand attracts guests to the properties for their first stays, sustainable, long-term profitability relies on customer loyalty. Using the balanced scorecard, Hilton was able to deliver a 3% higher profit margin than other full-service hotels. Between 2000 and 2002, this translated to a 100% increase in stock price.

Non-financial measures such as customer satisfaction, likelihood to recommend Hilton, and likelihood to return to Hilton have improved as well. Hilton has bettered the price-value relationship at its properties while raising its room rates, so guests have not fallen away from the brand despite increases to the cost of their stays.

At a strategic level, use of the balanced scorecard also has increased brand equity by reinforcing quality control of the Hilton experience. These diagnostic successes meant that Hilton Garden Inns, from launch, could command premium rates over competitors.[2]

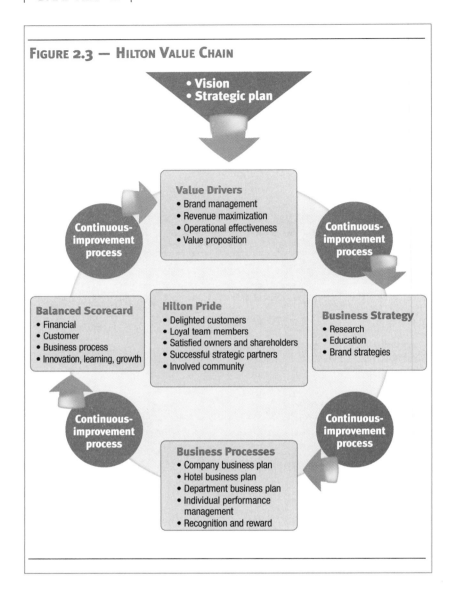

FIGURE 2.3 — HILTON VALUE CHAIN

- **Vision**
- **Strategic plan**

Value Drivers
- Brand management
- Revenue maximization
- Operational effectiveness
- Value proposition

Continuous-improvement process

Continuous-improvement process

Balanced Scorecard
- Financial
- Customer
- Business process
- Innovation, learning, growth

Hilton Pride
- Delighted customers
- Loyal team members
- Satisfied owners and shareholders
- Successful strategic partners
- Involved community

Business Strategy
- Research
- Education
- Brand strategies

Continuous-improvement process

Continuous-improvement process

Business Processes
- Company business plan
- Hotel business plan
- Department business plan
- Individual performance management
- Recognition and reward

CONCLUSION

So, where are you on the Ladder of Insight? Using this framework, you can begin to look at the next steps up the levels of measurement proficiency so you can identify which stage your company is in and what the next steps up the Ladder of Insight might look like. That perspective will help you envision what you want your dashboard to do for you and allow you to map out the stages of progression you would like to see it go through over time.

Seeing the road ahead will help deliver a more practical dashboard that's equipped to take you where you want to go, not just show you where you are today.

Sources

1. *MarketingNPV Journal*, vol. 1, issue 2.

2. *MarketingNPV Journal*, vol. 1, issue 6.

EVA is a registered trademark of Stern Stewart & Co.

Align Your Dashboard Right from the Start

M ost of us have a pretty keen ability to look backward and know where we've been. Many of us have even advanced that skill to be able to look around and know where we are at the moment. But knowing whether you're on track for where you expect to be six, 12, 18 months from now … that's something only a very few managers have mastered.

Today, marketing reporting, and to some degree financial reporting, is primarily a function of gathering sales data at the end of a reporting period, massaging it into charts and graphs, and then circulating it for discussion or comment. And for most, even this is no small accomplishment.

This diagnostic approach is rooted in the instinctive human learning method of interpreting past experiences to frame future expectations. At best, that process is effective at helping the organization see where it's recently been. Only through very intuitive methods do companies attempt to project the trajectory of performance into the future so they can manage to the desired outcome. And only a very few managers possess the innate (or artistic) ability to properly view diagnostic information and project it with reasonable accuracy, overcoming their own perceptual filters and assimilating the collective wisdom of their entire team.

Add to that the marketer's DNA being built more historically on spending money than making money and you can understand why marketers have very well-developed rear-view skills.

This is the fundamental human frailty dashboards are designed to overcome.

Without a doubt, there is benefit to having diagnostic measurements on your dashboard. But without components that help you predict the future, the dashboard is only expanding the limitations of memory, not improving decision making.

Think again about the dashboard on your car and how it works with your vision and stored experiences. You keep your eyes fixed on the road ahead with only quick glances at the dashboard to see how speed, fuel level, and engine stress will affect the desired outcome of arriving at your destination. Your brain makes millions of calculations per second to adjust the turn of the wheel, the pressure on the gas pedal, and the search for rest areas along the way. You might even have reviewed a map before starting out to form a mental picture in your mind of where you were going.

Today's vehicles are increasingly equipped with some "forward-looking" dashboard capabilities. Compasses are being replaced by GPS systems that provide real-time mapping to guide you to your destination, alerting you in advance to upcoming turns. Fuel gauges are evolving to become distance-to-empty meters that display not just the current level of the tank, but how far you can go before stopping based on average fuel economy. These advances make driving easier and more efficient. However, most marketing dashboard metrics are still being presented in the form of current vs. prior period. That's helpful in terms of seeing the trend to the current point in time. But, to use the vehicular metaphor, it would be like driving forward while looking in the rear-view mirror — more than a little dangerous.

Depicting historical trends has only one purpose — to improve the accuracy of predicting where you are likely to be in the future. Consequently, all of the metrics on a marketing dashboard should be compared to a *forecast* for where they're supposed to be at that point in time relative to the longer-term goals. That way, the dashboard answers the question, "Where is my projected outcome vs. my target outcome?"

FIGURE 3.1 — BACKWARD-LOOKING VS. FORWARD-LOOKING

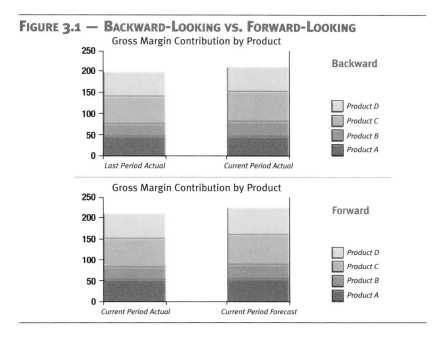

Proper marketing dashboard readings give you an indication of whether you're on the right course, at the right speed, and have enough gas in your tank to get to your *desired* destination, not just any destination. If the dashboard says you're off course, you can look at past-performance data for diagnostic insights and ideas on how to course-correct, but no longer will looking back be your central focus. A well-designed dashboard will always be looking ahead.

But before your forward-looking dashboard can take shape, you need to be certain that your destination and your desired outcomes are calibrated with those of senior management and the company overall.

Identifying the Right Destinations

Step #1: Aligning Marketing Goals with the Organization

In Chapter 1, we talked about the path to credibility — alignment, measurement, objectivity, and accountability are the key steps toward credibility with senior management.

Strategy mapping, an approach developed by Robert S. Kaplan and David P. Norton[1] (inventors of the balanced scorecard) is one way to kick off that process. You can use a strategy map to align marketing's goals with the rest of the organization and in the process define the role of marketing and the critical dimensions of creating the right customer value propositions. It's the first step toward selecting the right metrics for what will eventually become your marketing dashboard.

FIGURE 3.2 — SAMPLE STRATEGY MAP #1

Source: Adapted from Strategy Maps by Robert S. Kaplan and David P. Norton, Harvard Business School, 2004. Reprinted with permission.

Figure 3.2 shows the relationships among:

- the company's financial objectives;
- the strategies intended to achieve them;
- the customer value proposition(s) required to execute the strategies;
- the business processes required to deliver on the value proposition(s);
- the information management systems to support the business processes; and
- the organizational skills, structures, and culture necessary to pursue the objectives successfully.[2]

Financial objectives always boil down to growth in profits and appreciation of tangible and intangible assets — brands, customer relationships, distribution channels, etc. — which add up to overall shareholder value. While your specific metrics will vary, it's important to place highest-order financial goals at the top of the map.

The strategies intended to achieve these goals can be very customized and circumstantial, but they are normally some variation on the themes of:

- **Product/service leadership:** Being the best product or service in your field. Think Lexus, Armani, or Dell.

- **Niche domination:** When you're so close to the needs of a sub-segment of a market that you obtain competitive advantage in uniquely satisfying it. Gymboree Play & Music won over the high-end preschooler moms interested in an indoor experience for kids with more personal attention and nicer facilities than the local YMCA.

- **Customer convenience:** The ability to leverage customer relationships to cross-sell deeply. Verizon, for example, bundles local, long-distance, and wireless phone service with Internet service in a single bill to create a barrier to exit.

- **Low-cost position:** Engineer cost reduction so far below competitors that price becomes the defensible differentiator. Wal-Mart has this strategy perfected.

The customer value proposition is really the core of the strategy map. Its purpose is to move customers to behave as you would like them to — trying your product or service, extending their relationships with you, or remaining loyal to you in the face of competitors. The customer value proposition often mixes elements of pricing, quality, brand image, distribution, feature, and function to successfully leverage the company's strengths or exploit competitive weaknesses.

Achieving the desired customer value proposition often depends upon strong business processes in several supporting areas of operations, including product development, customer service, and regulatory or social issues management. These processes guide the organization to focus and execute on the things most directly required for success.

Undoubtedly, most of these critical processes will have as baseline needs some form of information management platform — not just the technical pieces of computers and data networks, but the way information is shared and used around the company. Most often, these platforms go beyond internal process facilitation, reaching outside of the company to suppliers, distributors, and, in some cases, customers.

The organizational elements of the *right* skills, structure, and cultural characteristics set the foundation for the successful delivery of information management, process, customer value proposition, strategy, and financial objectives. Without these well-developed organizational basics, no amount of gymnastics at higher levels will deliver consistently on the company strategy.

The strategy map helps to clarify marketing objectives and priorities. It also helps to identify the relationships between traditional marketing intermediary measures (brand awareness and equities, product trial, customer retention and satisfaction, distribution, etc.) and the ultimate business results of revenues, profits, and shareholder value.

FIGURE 3.3 — SAMPLE STRATEGY MAP #2

Financial Objectives

Increase profits from current customers by $100 million

Generate $85 million pretax profit from new sectors

Strategic Goals

Dominate DIY sectors
- share of $
- share of tickets
- relative price

Lowest cost per unit in-service
- $ to shelf
- lifetime service cost

Own "preferred provider" role
- brand tracker surveys

No. 1 volume installer within two years
- share of $
- customer satisfaction
- installer turnover

Customer Value Proposition

Superior quality products
- cost per 1,000
- survey perceptions

Easy-to-use
- support calls
- user surveys
- test lab comparisons

"Most trusted" brand
- brand tracker survey
- ad copy recall
- independent press mentions

Service value
- awareness of offer
- dealer inquiries
- close rates
- referral rates

Process Requirements

Product development
- feature popularity
- latest styles/materials
- consumer lab testing
- dealer lab testing

Operations
- shelf display
- in-stock hours
- inventory turns

Customer service
- CSR recruitment
- training progression
- first-call resolutions

Dealer development
- dealer identification
- contract completion
- training completion
- capacity forecast

IT upgrades required: online defect database; self-service Web site; customer comment action systems; dealer locator database; referral database; CSR cockpit speed

Skills
- create service line mgmt.
- expand pricing expertise

Structure
- add new service group
- share support functions

Culture
- increase variable % of comp.
- emphasize consumer contact

Organizational Needs

Figure 3.3 might represent a company that manufactures products purchased directly and installed or assembled by end users. The blue bullet points under each of the process, value proposition, and strategy components are possible metrics that could give shape to a marketing dashboard. It may also help clarify the role of marketing within the organization, which is important in developing a truly effective dashboard.

Step #2: Identifying Critical Performance Metrics Based on the Role of Marketing in Your Company

By now we've all heard about the Spencer Stuart survey that found that the average CMO's tenure is about 22 months — hardly long enough to see any major initiative through.[3] The key toward longevity, however, may be setting a role for the marketing department that fits the goals of the CEO.

A 2004 study by the Association of National Advertisers and Booz Allen Hamilton suggests that CMO success is first and foremost a function of knowing what role you're signing up for.[4] They suggested that there are three different roles of marketing organizations within companies.

Role #1: A Marketing Services Organization

The marketing department is a service provider to the rest of the organization. It provides the benefits of centralization in:
- media buying;
- advertising and marcomm materials development and production; and
- coordination of vendors and agencies.

Role #2: The Marketing Department as Advisor

As a corporate marketing function, the marketing department helps align marketing plans of multiple business units with overall corporate strategies in terms of:
- brand development, uniformity, and compliance;
- best-practice sharing across business units; and
- training/education to improve the breadth and depth of marketing skills throughout the company.

Role #3: Marketing as Growth Driver

The marketing department is the engine of growth for the CEO in driving the corporate agenda; it is responsible for alignment of all necessary resources including:

- brand strategy and execution;
- customer touchpoint and customer experience management;
- product development and innovation;
- customer value development; and
- marketing accountability and ROI.

FIGURE 3.4 — THREE BASIC ROLES FOR MARKETING[5]

Marketing Services	Marketing Advisor	Growth Driver
Service provider to the rest of the organization. Provides benefits of centralization in:	Leader of a corporate marketing function who helps align divisional marketing plans with corporate strategies:	Partner with CEO in driving corporate growth agenda; responsible for alignment of all necessary resources:
■ Media buying ■ Marcomm materials ■ Coordinating vendors and agencies	■ Brand compliance ■ Best-practice sharing ■ Training/education	■ Brand strategy ■ Customer touchpoints ■ Business development ■ Innovation ■ Marketing accountability and ROI

There may be other models or hybrids of the ones above. Regardless, knowing what role marketing is playing in pursuit of the company objectives and confirming it with the CEO and the rest of the executive committee sets the boundaries of the playing field on which marketing is expected to perform. In the process, it suggests some clear opportunities for important dashboard metrics.

Once you have better clarity on how marketing fits into the company strategy map and once you've confirmed the role of marketing in the organization, you need to identify the critical performance objectives for the marketing organization. It's impossible to build a relevant dashboard without knowing what those objectives are.

A good performance objective has three components: direction, magnitude, and timeframe.

Here's an example: "I will achieve a 20% increase in market share in the next 12 months." Increasing market share is the direction.

Twenty percent is the magnitude. Twelve months is the timeframe. If you take any one of those three components away, you're left with an ineffective statement of objectives open to subjective interpretation. If you take away the magnitude and just say, "I'm going to increase market share," you have no way to judge how much money you should invest in trying to achieve your goal or how much risk (i.e., spending) you should undertake to do so. If you take away the timeframe and just say you're going to achieve a 20% market share increase, you might be thinking that five years is a reasonable timeframe, while the CEO is thinking one year.

The three parts of a critical performance objective force you to close all the doors of subjectivity. And much like building a dashboard on forecast vs. "rear window," the process forces you to really think about what exactly it is that you plan to accomplish and how well your strategies and tactics are aligned to do so.

It's also fairly apparent how the three specific dimensions of critical objectives establish some potentially important candidates for dashboard metrics.

The next step is to see how well the tactics, programs, and activities are aligned with the strategy map and critical objectives.

Step #3: Resource Mapping

Another effective way to begin identifying the right marketing dashboard metrics is to graphically map out the "many-to-many" relationships between marketing goals, objectives, and tactics/initiatives. The simple process of deciding what are goals vs. objectives vs. tactics brings all marketing department activity into focus, exposing gaps and redundancies for the benefit of resource reallocation and continuous improvement.

Each tactic, program, or initiative should have its own success metric for determining if the investment achieved the desired result. As drivers of successful outcomes, these success metrics then become predictive candidates for inclusion in the dashboard.

But what if you have too many? How can you determine which ones matter most? Obviously we don't want a dashboard with dozens or hundreds of metrics diluting focus from the most important ones.

FIGURE 3.5 — RELATIONSHIP MAP BETWEEN MARKETING GOALS, OBJECTIVES, AND TACTICS/INITIATIVES

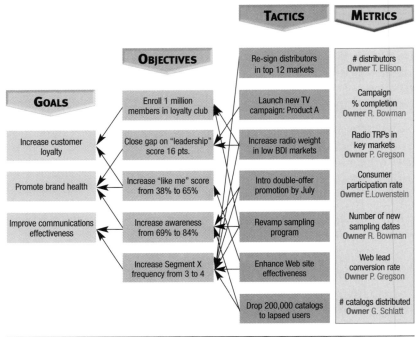

One way to filter many candidate metrics to fewer, more insightful selections is to weight the contribution of each tactic to the achievement of objectives and each objective to the attainment of goals. Analytical techniques can help establish these relative weightings if data is available. However, it's more likely that you'll need to discuss and debate the weightings as a group to build consensus on which elements of the map really drive results. The tactics with the greater weightings are the ones most likely to drive desired outcomes and thereby the best prospects for predictive dashboard metrics.

This approach often stimulates conflict among owners of competing initiatives, so you may want to undertake this with the help of some impartial facilitation. Eventually it will build extraordinary alignment on your marketing team — focusing your priorities in a way your department has never seen. And along the way, you might find that some of your tactics investments are "orphans" — they really don't line up well with any of the objectives you've set. That discovery is actually a great opportunity to reallocate money. Switch off those orphans and shift dollars to initiatives aligned with priority goals.

It is not uncommon to find that the first pass at the resource map shows that all the tactics are mapped back to all or most of the objectives, which suggests that either the purpose of each initiative is not very clearly defined, or that the relationships among goals, objectives, and tactics are not sufficiently distinct.

FIGURE 3.6 — COMPARING RESOURCE ALIGNMENT

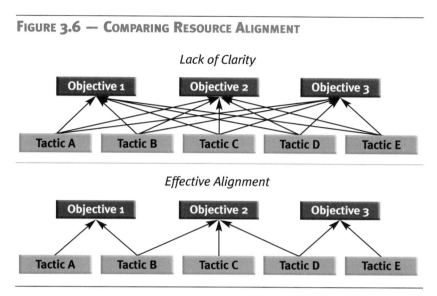

Either way, these outcomes are signs that there is significant room for improvement in clarifying exactly what you are trying to accomplish and how you are pursuing it. All of which is important spadework before designing your marketing dashboard.

Step #4: Test Causal Relationships

Once you have clarity on the relationships among tactics, objectives, and goals, testing causal relationships can help identify the very best predictive metrics for your dashboard.

Of course, the only way to truly prove that a given marketing initiative drove profitable sales is to establish a pure test vs. control experimental design in which all other variables are accounted for, leaving only the marketing stimulus to explain the change in sales.

Unfortunately, this is most often an impractical way to measure large-scale marketing in a world in which network TV purchases are more efficient than spot buys, and environmental and competitive forces are impolitely adding variables faster than you can control them. But there are ways to get some insight from which to draw conclusions.

Many large marketing organizations have already invested in sophisticated media- or marketing-mix models that use complex statistical regression techniques to isolate the contributory value of various marketing stimuli in achieving sales or profits. In effect, these models take into account the marketing activities by day or week and compare them to actual sales to find correlations between cause and effect. In some cases, these models are quite comprehensive, incorporating not only advertising by media, but direct marketing, channel initiatives, and all other tactical components of the marketing plan. In others, only the media elements (TV vs. print vs. radio vs. direct mail) are covered by the model, with many other tactics operating outside the spectrum of analysis.

Even with such a mix model, it is still quite difficult to prove pure correlation between marketing investment and sales. Often, the outputs from the models indicate that there are some clear relative winners between various marketing-mix elements — e.g., radio might prove much more correlated to sales results than outdoor advertising — leading you to fine tune your resource allocation by media. But you still don't really know just how much the overall advertising effort drove sales as distinct from the simultaneous influence of channel pricing, customer service experience, current events, or competitive promotions. Factor in the impact of creative effectiveness, weather patterns, or media stories, and you wind up with correlations that at best tend to be in the middle range of certainty, leaving open significant doors of doubt for finance to step through and reject your analysis. In fact, it's not uncommon for mix models to explain only 15% to 25% of the variance in sales or margin, leaving the balance to be considered as "base" sales — presumably those that would have occurred even without the marketing stimulus.

The point is, these models can be quite helpful in "answering" the question, "Is marketing generating incremental profit?" However, they're not particularly effective at answering the CEO's real question: "Should I spend half as much as I do today on marketing or twice as much?"

To get that answer, you need to employ a series of measurement processes to identify the real drivers of marketing effectiveness, including:

- panel studies of customers and prospects, recording their progression through the sales funnel over time in relationship to marketing activities;

- continual survey research among samples of the target audience to gauge the impact of marketing investments individually or collectively on the relative shifts in purchase consideration or behavior from one period to the next; and

- econometric models of customer behavior from transaction files to measure the changes in the collective value of the customer base in response to marketing activities.

While each of these methods can play a role in gathering insight about what works and what doesn't, there is no silver bullet. Sometimes, the best strategy is to gather the preponderance of evidence from multiple measurement approaches to identify the elements of the marketing plan that are *most likely* driving future financial outcomes, and then constantly test the insights gained to get more accurate at predicting the outcome of a change in an element of the marketing stimulus package.

This is precisely the role the marketing dashboard should play — helping you graphically correlate learnings from multiple sources into an overall picture of marketing effectiveness designed to facilitate the asking of good questions more than the answering of unanswerable ones.

Making your dashboard predictive takes time. It requires that the marketing organization put sound measurement processes into place and then use them to continually challenge long-held assumptions about what works and why. Eventually, over time, you learn to focus in on the things that are most likely to be predictive and prove their accuracy. Most often, this turns out to be the discovery of several predictive components, none of which are perfectly reliable, but when viewed collectively are accurate the vast majority of times.

Remember, the dashboard is intended to continually present you with evidence of your ignorance. By constantly comparing actual results to forecast, you are forced to continuously improve your forecasting ability and learn from each day's new errors. It's supposed to make you a less fallible human, not Merlin the Magician. Keep pushing the limits of your human powers to identify the root-cause elements of success. These are the best candidates for truly predictive dashboard metrics.

If you completely lack any data or the budget for research, fear not. In Chapter 8, you'll see some helpful tools for uncovering causal relationships when analytics aren't an option.

FIVE WAYS TO IMPROVE THE QUALITY OF YOUR FORECASTING

"It's tough to make predictions, especially about the future."
— Yogi Berra

Even if you're still working with a No. 2 pencil and scrap paper, there's no reason you can't produce outstanding quality forecasts with more predictability and reliability than you've ever experienced before.

While advanced mathematics and enormous computational power have improved significantly, few would argue that forecasting is an exact science. That's because at its core, forecasting is still mostly a human dynamic in which accuracy is dependent upon:

- asking the right people the right questions;
- the willingness of those people to answer truthfully and completely;
- the ability of the forecaster to separate the meaningful elements from the noise; and
- the openness of the forecaster to suggestions of process improvement.

That last point is key: process improvement. Consistently good forecasting isn't a mathematical exercise performed at regular intervals (e.g., quarterly) as much as it's an ongoing process of gathering and evaluating dozens or hundreds of points of information into a decision framework. Then, when called upon (e.g., quarterly), this decision framework can output the best forward-looking view grounded in the insights of the contributors. While software can facilitate process structure by prompting for specific fields of information to be included, it cannot make judgments on the quality of the information being input. As we've said, "Garbage in; garbage out."

1. Be Specific

As simple as this sounds, knowing exactly what you are forecasting is the most important step to success. It might seem pretty obvious that if you want to forecast sales, forecast sales. But what question are you really trying to answer? Unit sales? Gross margin? Market share? Customer value?

Also, what period of time do you need to cover? The longer out the forecast goes, the less reliable it is in the out years. This becomes especially important if your forecast is intended to anticipate the market size of a new category that will cost tens of millions or more to enter.

In general, forecasts fall into one of two categories: operational and strategic. Operational forecasts manage the existing organization one or two steps ahead of today's reality. Strategic forecasts look further out into the future to help focus the company's long-range planning. In mature market categories (toothpaste, personal computers, pet foods, etc.), the operational time horizon could be two to five years and the strategic 10 or more.

2. Be Structured

There are many reasons to take a structured, methodical approach to forecasting. First and most obvious is the importance of not leaving out key information that might affect the forecast. Also, there is the quality control factor and the benefit of double- and triple-checking all the assumptions and formulas. But among the less obvious benefits of structure are:

- the removal of personal biases that might unknowingly be causing participants to filter their inputs or interpretations;
- the continuity of consistently improving upon the process over time, regardless of turnover among key input or executional resources;
- the auditability of the approach to determine where things might have gone awry at various steps in the process; and
- the confidence your rigor will inspire when others evaluate your work and are by necessity forced to accept some subjective judgments and assumptions.

Structure needn't be costly or time-consuming. In its simplest form, it is taking the time to map out and document all the inputs into the forecasting process; describing (in writing) the apparent relationships between causal factors; noting all assumptions and calculations in an easily referenced manner; and recording the accuracy of the resulting forecasts over time, alongside observations on emerging factors that might have influenced the results.

3. Be Quantitative — with or without "Data"

If you have lots of historical data at hand, quantitative fore-casting methods such as moving averages, time-series analysis, and exponential smoothing create a much greater likelihood of developing a strong forecast, provided you have enough historical data to use them. But even if the only data you have are a series of "finger-in-the-air" estimates, you can still take a more disciplined quantitative approach by building simulations that explore the "what-if" scenarios often hidden in best guesses at average outcomes.

Regardless of the quantitative approach you use, keep in mind that like power tools, mathematics can be really dangerous in the hands of the inexperienced. Hiring someone with strong statistical skills to determine the most appropriate quantitative method(s), given your data (or lack thereof), provides yet another comparison point to check against your experiential judgment.

Even if you choose to disregard the forecast derived by crunching the numbers, at least the exercise caused you to think about your instincts a bit harder. More likely, the quantitative process will raise questions about assumptions and data anomalies, which will highlight previously overlooked risks relevant to the forecast.

4. Be More Than Quantitative — Find Causal Factors

Straight statistical extrapolation is fine for simple situations with short time horizons. But more variables can affect the forecast over a longer horizon. The factors most likely to influence the forecast need to be identified and their possible impacts assessed as closely as they can be.

Sometimes causal factors can be obvious. For example, when forecasting anticipated growth in sales of sunglasses, one should take into account weather forecasts, since abnormally sunny or rainy weather can dramatically influence consumer purchase behavior. Other times, if you look more closely, causal relationships aren't so obvious, which is why you wouldn't normally guess that Seattle is the No.1 market in America for sunglasses per capita. Seattle? Rainy, overcast Seattle? It turns out that since the sunshine is far less frequent, people have a habit of losing their sunglasses between uses and need to constantly buy new ones.

The first step in identifying causal factors is to convene an "expert panel" of people from within your organization who possess several years of experience. Supplement the panel with suppliers, channel partners, or leading academics in the field and ask them to identify and rank the things that tend to make sales go up or down. Try to translate the responses into definitions of factors for which there are historical measures — like weather, industry sales of complementary products, medical conditions, etc. Where necessary, look for proxy measures that might be reasonably good approximations of the real factor — like population growth is a proxy for demand for haircuts.

Once you've identified some potential causal factors or proxies, again look to statistical methods like regression models to test the extent to which the causal factor is truly causal (e.g., is directly or inversely related to actual historical sales). Allow the quantitative process to remove any personal bias about which factors might be most causal. Also allow it to eliminate causal elements that are linked and, thereby, redundant.

Many forecasting experts agree that evaluating the results from multiple forecasting approaches is indeed the best way to ensure that you have the fullest perspective on the possible outcomes. Armed with that perspective, you can apply your experience and instinct to determining the most likely forecast scenario.

5. K.I.S.S.

As with most things in life, simplicity is a virtue in forecasting. Einstein said, "Things should be made as simple as possible, but no simpler." In forecasting, we interpret that to mean that an accurate and reliable forecasting process should be comprehensive enough to identify the truly causal factors, but simple enough to explain to those who will need to make decisions upon it.[6]

Tips on Forecasting with Existing Data

There are dozens of ways to forecast from historical data (see more in Chapter 8). The type of forecast you are making and the number and nature of the causal variables will determine which of the many statistical techniques are most appropriate to your forecasting challenge.

As a marketing manager, you don't need to know the merits of regression, exponential smoothing, Box-Jenkins, or other statistical methods. What you do need is a Ph.D. consultant or university professor to test a broad range of methods against your historical data to determine which methods are most accurate and/or most practical for your forecasting needs.

Once you have selected the appropriate statistical methodology for your forecast, you can choose from numerous inexpensive PC-based forecasting tools that can crunch the data fast, speeding up your forecasting process. The benefit of carefully selecting and then sticking with an automated software tool is that you begin to build consistent forecasting processes and measurement benchmarks. (It also doesn't hurt to have one in place when the CEO asks you to have a revised forecast of unit sales by country under three pricing scenarios on his desk that afternoon.)

You don't have to be a rocket scientist to select and use a tool. Today's forecasting tools are built to be used by decision makers, not quants. For the most part, they have friendly interfaces and drag-and-drop actions to run the program. There are some 40-plus desktop forecasting tools on the market that range from simple Excel plug-in modules to sophisticated software packages, priced from $50 to $5,000-plus. But don't expect a "plug-and-play" experience. These tools all require some degree of a learning curve and familiarity with statistics. If you're just starting out, you might want to stick with the basic spreadsheet approach.

There is no power in a forecast if those who need to trust it cannot understand or explain the logic and process behind it. Recognizing forecasting to be a complex human decision process is the first step toward dramatically improving your batting average and improving the accuracy and reliability of the forecasts coming out of your department.

CONCLUSION

Preparing your organization to isolate the right kind of metrics for your dashboard starts with a mission of self-discovery. Don't be concerned with lack of data or analytical skills. Many of the most important questions to answer can be discussed around a conference room table, leading to greater clarity and focus on what's really paramount.

Remember, it's particularly important not to bite off more than you can chew in the initial effort — don't go for quantity of metrics, go for finding a select few of the most informative, forward-looking measurements that fit your organization and reflect your clarity on the role of marketing in helping the company meet its stated goals.

Sources

1. Kaplan, Robert S. and Norton, David P., *Strategy Maps*, Harvard Business School Press, 2004.

2. *MarketingNPV Journal*, vol. 1, issue 6.

3. Welch, Greg, Spencer Stuart, "CMO Tenure: Slowing Down the Revolving Door," July 2004.

4. ANA (Association of National Advertisers) and Booz Allen Hamilton, "Are CMOs Irrelevant? Organization, Value, Accountability, and the New Marketing Agenda," 2004.

5. *MarketingNPV Journal*, vol. 2, issue 1.

6. *MarketingNPV Journal*, vol. 1, issue 3.

PART II

What Do We Measure? Choosing the Right Metrics for Your Dashboard

Develop an "ROI" Framework: Key First Steps to Identifying the Right Dashboard Metrics

There's very little sense in creating a great, forward-looking dashboard for a poorly designed automobile. By that, we mean that a marketing dashboard is useless — without the solid mechanics of profitability management behind it.

Actually, that might be overstating it a bit. You can certainly *create* a dashboard without this infrastructure — it just won't be worth much. This is exactly what we see time and again: Eager dashboard builders create elaborately layered charts and graphs of metrics that don't really provide any insight into the underlying causes affecting their business or the trajectory they're unknowingly committed to.

This chapter will zero in on two concepts necessary to bring the underlying discipline of profitability management into your marketing organization: funnel management and profit optimization. Together, they create a framework for measuring and improving marketing effectiveness. If they already exist in your company, dashboard construction will be primarily a methodical design exercise. If they do not, you have some work to do before you begin thinking about what your dashboard will look like.

Funnel management provides a structure for learning how awareness translates to attitudes, attitudes to preferences, preferences to behaviors, and behaviors to profits. It is a simple and efficient tool that blends the classic advertising "hierarchy of effects" model with elements of strategic sales management. Funnel management takes a large group of potential prospects and defines the stages through which the group is transformed into a valuable selection of dedicated customers. Using such a tool allows marketing professionals the opportunity to monitor almost daily progress toward measurable profits.

FIGURE 4.1 — THE MARKETING FUNNEL

One of marketing's key objectives is to produce specific consumer or customer behaviors that lead to positive financial outcomes. A marketing program or initiative may have a specific purpose in moving prospects through one stage of the funnel — such as building brand preference or generating qualified leads. But these marketing investments only pay back when incremental profits are derived at the end of the funnel. We can create huge numbers of aware brand disciples in the marketplace, but if they're not buying from us (at profitable prices), the investment is wasted. This is why it is so critical to identify and plug the leaks in the funnel.

There's no practical way to build a 100% leak-proof funnel process. At each stage of the funnel, some prospects or customers will leak out as their needs or circumstances change or competitive entreaties lure them away from you. Nevertheless, the goal of funnel management is clear: Plug the leaks. When you find and plug leaks, you create incremental profits. If only one out of every 100 prospects who become aware of your product buy it, you have 99% leakage, or waste. Even if some of that spending is expected to pay back in the form of latent customer conversions, understanding and plugging the leaks can substantially improve the return you derive from your investments in getting prospects into the top of the funnel.

Linking the marketing portion of the funnel to the sales portion is an excellent way to map and test the relationships between marketing's efforts at brand development and demand generation, and the sales force's ability to take that demand and turn it into profitable customer relationships. Too often, companies separate marketing from sales, creating a "handoff" mentality in which each department believes it is doing its part, but the other is not pulling its weight.

FIGURE 4.2 — INTEGRATED MARKETING/SALES FUNNEL

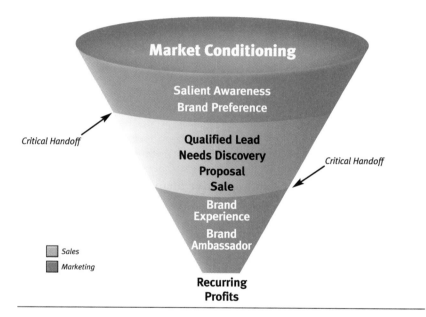

An integrated funnel (figure 4.2) provides an informative view of marketing performance at all stages. It represents the progression from unaware prospects to profitable "brand ambassadors." It also begins to dissect the process to enable linkage analysis in the search for correlations of how success in generating progress through certain stages of the funnel leads to further progression.

Once those links become clear, strategies and tactics can more easily be aligned and targeted to specific stages of funnel progression in which the effect would maximize impact from marketing investments. One way to measure this impact is using ROI.

The simple formula for calculating ROI is:

$$ROI = \frac{\text{NPV of Incremental Profits (Incremental Revenue − Expenses)}}{\text{Initial Expenses}}$$

"NPV" is the net present value of a series of profits realized over a period of time, discounted back to current dollars.

Many marketers and academics have denounced the use of an ROI formula in measuring marketing effectiveness as "too limiting" or possibly "misleading." We agree. Used in the wrong way or poorly manipulated, ROI calculations can be as imprecise and subject to misinterpretation as any other statistical or financial assessment tool. (See Expert View on the next page.)

However, when used properly in the context of driving more profit — not just getting the highest possible ROI score — ROI measurement is a reasonable way to standardize the process of gauging the *relative* value of one marketing investment against another.

If every marketing investment is held to the standard of ultimately creating some profitable change in customer or market behavior, then we can successfully compare *all* proposed investments using a standardized assessment process to identify those offering the greatest potential for driving profits. Sure, we might need to make some assumptions, but if we place some significant effort on trying to anticipate the intended behavior changes upfront in the planning stages, we can often identify ways to better structure our investments to help promote reliable measurement of results. This in turn helps us see where our assumptions were accurate, where they were less so, and why. Over time, our assumptions get better and better in planning our investments and achieving maximum return.

A consistent framework for assessing marketing returns allows marketing executives to:
- identify places where spending is most effective;
- correlate the individual and collective impact of marketing initiatives on prospect or customer behaviors, then link those behaviors to the financial value drivers;

- reallocate people or dollar resources towards greater impact — for example, this can include taking an underperforming initiative and retargeting it toward a high-value segment, eliminating unprofitable channel gaps and addressing identified leaks in the funnel progression; and
- extend campaign-level profitability to customer-level profitability across multiple acquisition, retention, and cross-sell campaigns that will optimize customer value.

EXPERT VIEW: MARKETING MEASUREMENT

Tim Ambler
SENIOR FELLOW, LONDON BUSINESS SCHOOL

You're no fan of return on marketing investment (ROMI) as a metric are you?

AMBLER: *It's arithmetically flawed. If you're looking at the return from marketing, you would normally look to things such as net cash flow or shareholder value that subtract costs from revenue. But what ROMI does is divide revenue or profits by costs, and when you start dividing rather than subtracting, you open the door for some erroneous conclusions. For example, if you spend $1 million and generate $500,000 net incremental profit, you have a 50% ROI. But if you spend $100,000 and generate $200,000 incremental, you get a 200% ROI. Which is better for the company? ROI doesn't give you the whole picture. Free cash flow can be so much more important to most companies.*

Another concern is that marketers driven to increase ROMI can do so by cutting the "I," and that isn't generally an effective strategy for growth. ROI works when you have to make a choice between options that require the same amount of scarce capital and the choices are mutually exclusive. But discounted cash flow (DCF) would still be the preferred metric in such cases. Marketing is not a once-off capital sum (for which ROI was invented) but a continuous stream of expenditures which the company makes every year.

So are you advocating more of an NPV or DCF approach?

DCF is fine for measuring the future potential of any activity compared with another. Assuming you do DCF on a normal accounting basis, you are evaluating alternative marketing initiatives against each other on the basis of expected cash flows for the current year and for several years into the future. That's fine. But that is quite different from trying to evaluate the results of the marketing you've done up to the present time.

If you're looking at actual results, you want to know what has happened up until now. You don't want to confuse that with what might take place in the future. So you have to take the short-term profit you've achieved and see if your brand asset (I call it brand equity) has gone up, in which case you want to take even more credit for achieving both short-term profit and increase in brand assets. But if the brand assets have gone down, your short-term profits aren't viewed quite so positively. This is very important when looking at things like price promotions.

Are you suggesting that organizations need to do a much better job of defining their objectives upfront?

I think that's true, but that's not what people do. The biggest predictor of what will be in this year's marketing plan is whatever was in last year's marketing plan, not some change in objectives.

Short-term profit is fairly easy to benchmark against other investments the company might make. But how do you measure "brand equity," as you define it?

This is difficult. In a perfect world, it would be nice to value brand equity at its present value, because then you could express brand equity in short-term dollars. Unfortunately, you can't do that. You need to look at a dashboard of key brand equity measures and be broad-minded enough to accept multiple components of your assessment instead of a single financial number — with the idea that a dashboard gives you a better idea of what the state of your marketing activity is.

That sounds like an approach intended to increase confidence in marketing's "accountability" vs. one intended to specifically measure return.

Yes, and therein lies the challenge when it comes to explaining how marketing really works to non-marketing people, particularly financial people. The financial people would like everything measured in dollars (as we all would), but it's just not practical. You would need to make too many assumptions along the way and the validity of your ultimate numbers would be suspect at best. Now, I'm all for marketing people becoming as financially literate as possible, but the financial people must become more marketing literate as well. And it comes back to the point about setting objectives. If the financial people are involved in the marketing planning process, as they should be, then they will come to understand that the dashboard is really the only way to do it.[1]

Mapping the Funnel

One of the most important roles for marketing is to motivate prospects to progress through stages in the funnel. The funnel tracks changes in customer behavior that result from a single activity or series of marketing activities to sales, which are then linked to financial outcomes. On your dashboard, this will be reflected in terms of:

- understanding where marketing performance is succeeding versus failing; and

- establishing links between funnel stages to help predict future outcomes.

FIGURE 4.3 — SAMPLE MARKETING/SALES FUNNEL

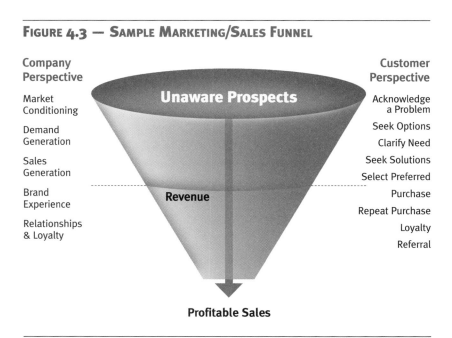

Company Perspective

- Market Conditioning
- Demand Generation
- Sales Generation
- Brand Experience
- Relationships & Loyalty

Unaware Prospects

Revenue

Customer Perspective

- Acknowledge a Problem
- Seek Options
- Clarify Need
- Seek Solutions
- Select Preferred
- Purchase
- Repeat Purchase
- Loyalty
- Referral

Profitable Sales

The marketing and sales funnel in figure 4.3 represents progressive stages that targeted prospects may pass through from initial awareness to forming an opinion to purchasing and then conducting an ongoing relationship with the company.

On the left side of the funnel is the company perspective of the progression path. On the right, there is the prospect/customer perspective. At corresponding points in each path, "interest" turns into a sale and economic value is created.

We could go into great depth of detail on what the various stages of funnel progression might look like, but first it might be helpful to have some background on these progression pathways.

Over 100 years ago, marketers first conceived a model for consumer purchasing behavior. Originally, it was suggested to be a very simple model of four stages:

Awareness ➤ Interest ➤ Desire ➤ Action

Conventional wisdom was that the consumer followed this progression in deciding what to purchase and when.

In the 1960s, the HOE (hierarchy of effects) model was developed upon the assumption of a three-stage process in consumer behavior:

Cognition ➤ Affect ➤ Behavior

"Cognition" represented the process of becoming specifically aware of a solution to fit one's need; "affect" was the process of becoming emotionally engaged in the purchase; and "behavior" was the resulting purchase.

Over the past 40 years, all this has proven time and again to be *wrong*.

The HOE model may be right for some categories and some consumers at some points in time, but it fails miserably as a predictor of how most people buy in most categories most of the time. It assumes a sequential linearity of the buying process that just isn't true in many (if not most) occasions. True, you are unlikely to buy something you are not aware of. But, you might just become aware of it by seeing it on the shelf at the checkout counter and decide, on impulse, to pick it up. No emotional bonding required.

So why do we bring it up if it's so wrong?

The real value of the HOE model to marketers isn't in its accuracy as much as its existence. The mere fact that we have such a model as a starting point to begin to consider how our own categories work and what the linear or non-linear stages of progression might be among our own customers is highly beneficial in forcing us to think "outside-in" from the customer perspective. It encourages us to map out the models that work in our own business, see where the critical prospect/customer progressions might be, and better understand what causes those progressions to work or what obstacles prevent them.

The funnel we've been discussing here is likewise just a conceptual tool to map the process of how customers become customers. Prospects may progress through the entire funnel in less than a minute (someone choosing an impulse item off a crowded shelf in a retail outlet) or extend over several years (a business making a major technology investment).

Chances are that these funnels do *not* accurately describe your business and the way your customers buy. However, by now you hopefully understand that the challenge is to map out the one that *does* work for you.

The model in figure 4.3 shows one way that awareness turns into attitudes that translate into behaviors. It has never actually been proven to be a fully accurate view of what really happens between the consumers' ears, but *testing* its applicability to or limitations within your industry/product may illuminate some clear correlations, positive or negative, that should help you continue to refine your understanding of the pathway from awareness to purchase and repurchase.

Figure 4.4 shows another method of mapping the marketing and sales inputs into the customer buying process and links those to financial outcomes.

FIGURE 4.4 — MAP OF MARKETING AND SALES INPUTS INTO THE CUSTOMER BUYING PROCESS WITH LINKS TO FINANCIAL OUTCOMES

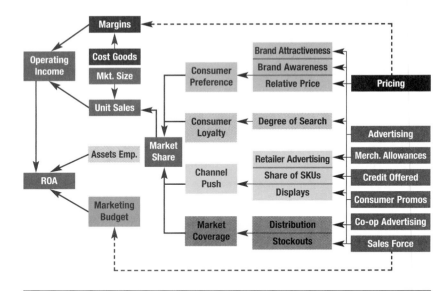

Source: Copyright © 2005 Dave Reibstein and Paul Farris, The Wharton School of the University of Pennsylvania. Reprinted with permission.[2]

This is a good example of the challenge most marketing departments need to undertake to better correlate marketing investments to business outcomes.

Regardless of what your "funnel" looks like, by the time you get to the bottom, only a small portion of the initial prospects actually convert into sales. Those who leak out along the way generally fall into one of two main categories:

1. the wrong target — someone highly unlikely to ever convert to a sale; or
2. a good prospect that your marketing efforts haven't yet won.

Generally speaking, profitability will improve if you spend less budget and effort on trying to prevent the "wrong target" types from leaving and more on improving your effectiveness against the "good prospects." Diagnosing the nature of leakage helps ensure that you don't focus too much spending at the top of the funnel, only to lose prospects later when you have no formalized program in place to hold on to them.

Leakage is a particular problem in organizations in which marketing generates leads that are handed off to sales. Marketing may dramatically improve its effectiveness in increasing lead volume, but if sales can't close more deals, the entire process is of little value to the company. The same gap can occur in an organization in which brand spending is effective at increasing salient awareness and strong brand preference, but the marketing initiatives intended to convert brand preference to actual sales are ineffective.

A closer look at why the marketing-sales handoff most often fails reveals the most likely causes:

- Marketing increases lead volume beyond sales capacity.
- Marketing increases lead volume with the wrong target — a group that has a low incidence of closing.
- Marketing and sales are not aligned on the key value propositions and communication strategies.
- Sales has other priorities and isn't working the leads provided by marketing.

To adequately diagnose the areas for greatest improvement, we need to break down the funnel into as many discrete stages as possible from both the company and the buyer's perspectives — with the latter being most important.

Mapping the funnel from the company's perspective is the typical approach that will make sense as we build strategic and tactical plans. But the classic "supply-chain" marketing models often overlook the subtleties of the demand process in the marketplace. Mapping the funnel from the buyer's perspective can be much more insightful, helping marketers to better understand the market forces behind conversion and leakage.

Mapping Your Funnel Step by Step

1. Map the funnel stages from the buyer's perspective for each important market segment that exhibits a unique buying process: Apply what knowledge you have of your industry/category, and be sure to highlight your assumptions for future investigation through research. Try to isolate each stage in prospecting and relationship development in which portions

of the audience might fail to progress and the underlying causes (see Chapter 8 for some good tools to apply here).

2. **Define key measurement points within the funnel:** The percentage of successful conversions from one stage to the next is known as the conversion rate. Tracking conversion rates is useful for projecting performance and identifying key profit improvement opportunities. It might be tempting to measure progression through every stage in the funnel with regular frequency, but realistically, you may be limited to select points along the way based on measurability or cost constraints. The most important points are critical gateways that tend to accelerate or restrict the pace of flow through the funnel. For example, a chemical company we know has found that once a prospect orders a sample of some new chemical product, that prospect is five times more likely to become a customer. Consequently, they know how much they can spend to generate a sample request and how much the sample request is worth in potential customer value. These key prediction points are the highlights of the funnel.

3. **Track progression through the funnel:** You can do this by measuring general movement of groups of prospects period over period (the "pig in the python" method) or by tracking individual customers with whom a direct relationship exists. Measurement methodologies include database analysis, panel studies, and quantitative research. Your funnel should factor in lag time so the progression performance can be fully reflected in projections.

4. **Establish linkage patterns:** Funnel management requires an understanding of how changes at one stage in the funnel are likely to affect future stages. For example, if a marketing initiative increases consideration and purchase intent, does that appear to translate into more sales meetings and higher close rates, or are additional tactical initiatives required? Start with observations from experience if that's all you have. You might use some facilitated sessions to capture the experiences of a group of marketing and sales personnel and make your collective assumptions off this "tribal knowledge." If you have data, statistical regression approaches provide the greatest

degree of certainty. The point is, work with what you have and refine your thinking. Then, put the continuous improvement process in place to get more reliable estimates over time.

5. **Monitor and validate projections:** Making assumptions based on past performance is all we have at the beginning, but it's important to realize that marketing performance is subject to continual change in dynamic markets. Be on the watch for changes in conversion and leakage throughout funnel progression so you can initiate corrective actions quickly.

CMO View: Understanding the Funnel

Joe Tripodi
Chief Marketing Officer
The Allstate Corporation

Lately, we've been working on "remixing" our marketing. Instead of spending 100% of our marketing dollars in the last year on very general brand messages that attack very broad segments of the marketplace, we're getting much more focused in regards to fine-tuning and refining our programming and call-to-action marketing. We want to determine more directly and overtly the relationship between the spend and the results.

Allstate isn't likely to transform fully into a Geico model of 100% direct response marketing. We're not going to go there, but we're certainly going to move a long way toward getting people to better understand that if we spend X, the result will be Y.

At the end of the day, when you look at the process for how we build the business, marketing is there at the top of the funnel, driving demand generation. We're not there in an agent's office, nor is anyone from the marketing department closing the sale. So, we work hard to get everybody to understand what their roles are in the overall funnel. If someone in the agent network says, "This advertising isn't working — it's not driving incremental sales," marketing needs to be able to say, "Well, wait a minute. Look at all the incremental 'quoting' that we drove." All this extra quote volume is a reflection of driving consumer demand. The inquiries are there, but the sales aren't closing. Are the quality of the leads good? If not, maybe the advertising is broken. Otherwise, we may be looking at a distribution system issue, not a marketing issue. Either way, it's important to find out fast and take the corrective actions.

From a process point of view, deconstructing the sales funnel and then getting everyone to understand their role is critically important to continuous improvement in our business.[3]

Strong Funnel Management Gives You:

- The baseline measures to assess how an event in one stage of the funnel will flow through to subsequent stages of the funnel, including the financial outcome. Supported with a structured measurement process, this type of analysis can guide budgeting based on the assumed results.

- An understanding of the lasting effect of funnel progression. If brand awareness or product interest is generated without follow up, at what point does that buyer's interest dissipate? Alternatively, if we believe that demand generation investments have a multi-year payout, the funnel helps us test that hypothesis and attempt to measure it specifically.

- Tighter integration of marketing tactics. The timing, message, and objective of each marketing tactic needs to be mapped to the funnel so that the performance of related programs can be assessed over independent initiatives to see if the whole is adding up to more than the sum of the parts.

Key Measurements from the Funnel That Feed into the Dashboard Include:

- actual progression rates from stage to stage;
- projected continued progression over future periods;
- expected profits from financial value drivers (tied to expected profits at the bottom of the funnel);
- cost per funnel progression; and
- frequency of leakage rates by reason.

Establishing an "ROI" Framework

Used appropriately, ROI can be one of the most helpful metrics for marketing. It illuminates the primary drivers of short-term financial performance from your current portfolio of marketing investments and allows you to prioritize future budget allocations. It also creates a means to manage risk — perhaps for the first time — in your marketing plan.

An effective ROI framework includes a detailed marketing and sales funnel, financially sound ROI calculations, and profit-driven strategic and tactical planning processes. This is how you begin to talk the language of your CFO. But getting there may not be easy.

A 2004 survey conducted by Forrester Research and the ANA found "a lack of consensus among marketers on how to measure/define their return on investment (ROI) in marketing."[4] The top choices were Incremental Sales Revenue Generated by Marketing Activities (66%) and Changes in Brand Awareness (57%). Other top choices referred to purchase intentions, attitudes, market share, and leads.

None of these are correct.

Is there a right answer to how marketing ROI is defined? Yes. If you were to ask individuals how they defined and measured the ROI on their stock portfolio, what kind of responses would you expect? Most investors will not be satisfied if their stock portfolio returns are defined as "most popular stocks" or "most likely to grow." They also won't be satisfied if they get high growth rates that are more than offset by high commission fees.

ROI is an efficiency measure built on incremental profits. Not revenue. Profits. It's about the return (in new profits) you get from investing past profits. Calculating ROI on anything other than profits is misleading at best, and *will* undermine your credibility amongst your peers in finance.

The first step in creating your ROI framework is to standardize the ROI calculation and define the data points used in that calculation. The formula must be constructed with complete financial integrity to meet the standards of the CFO and other executives outside of marketing. Return on investment provides the ratio of incremental profits generated to the proposed marketing investment. The investment and return must reflect the net present value (NPV) of the stream of future cash flows. Once again, the formula is:

$$\text{ROI} = \frac{\text{NPV of Incremental Profits (Incremental Revenue – Expenses)}}{\text{Initial Expenses}}$$

The ROI calculation should reflect the projected or actual impact of a specific marketing initiative you identified during funnel mapping. The marketing initiative may be a campaign, a subcomponent of a campaign, a series of integrated campaigns, or any initiative designed to profitably influence customer behaviors.

Remember that the goal is not to maximize ROI but to use ROI as a tool to maximize profits. Profitability is optimized for a marketing initiative when the point of diminishing returns is identified and the last dollar spent meets the threshold or hurdle rate set by the company.

To accomplish this, you must use a multilevel analysis consisting of independent, incremental, and aggregate ROI or NPV measures. The independent measure is done for a stand-alone marketing initiative at its smallest feasible design. From there, incremental measures are run as the target audience size is expanded, as new media channels are added, and/or as offers or other enhancements are made to the core initiative. An aggregate measure then encompasses the complete initiative and possibly multiple initiatives that together have a greater impact than when run independently. This multilevel approach is critical to reflecting the need for integrated campaigns to fully motivate prospects through the entire funnel.

Your financial model can exist in an Excel spreadsheet or more sophisticated software. You'll also have to figure out how to stream-line access to data. Critical business intelligence is also required. The goal is to simplify the process so marketers can input the known and assumed values of the initiative, project the return and assess alternative scenarios, and modify the strategic and tactical plans to reflect the highest profit potential.

At every stage, think about how the findings might eventually look on your dashboard. If you can't visualize the findings on a dashboard, ask yourself if you should really be doing these particular measurements.

The most challenging part of determining marketing effectiveness is often measuring the incremental impact that results from executing the marketing initiative. The key challenges include:

- identifying a reliable "baseline" of sales activity that would have resulted in the absence of marketing;
- getting access to necessary data;
- designing measurements that leverage the right mix of methodologies available;
- allocating the resources necessary for measurement and analysis; and
- establishing a measurement hierarchy based on profit potential.

The measurement hierarchy defines what gets measured, how often, through which methodology, and at what cost. This is done based on the reality that it is not practical or possible to measure everything. With the sales funnel and financial return model in place, you should know where the greatest profit impact exists and what measures will give the most insight. High priority measurements could include identification of customer-level profitability, assessing a specific media channel, optimizing a high frequency campaign, or measuring leakage rates at select points in the funnel.

The ideal measurement methodology is classic experimental design (test vs. control) in which the isolated independent variable can be proven to be the exclusive cause of changes in the ultimate outcome. Unfortunately, the conditions to conduct such pure tests are rarely present. So where marketplace realities complicate the assessment environment, marketing-mix modeling and agent-based modeling are popular approaches for assessing marketing performance. The former attempts to use statistical regression to find correlations between various elements of the marketing or media plan and the resulting sales or profits. The latter uses much more sophisticated multivariable techniques to measure the performance of entire markets and market segments in response to small changes in stimulus elements (marketing programs). There are also quantitative research surveys, panel studies, direct observations, and pre-/post-measurements. Strong measurement plans incorporate a blend of these methodologies.

Risk-Adjusted Returns

Globalization, multichannel marketing, supply-chain management, strategic alliances, regulations, corporate governance — marketing is riskier today than ever. To put their companies at competitive advantage, marketers need to take more calculated risks. Yet to most marketing departments, "risk management" is limited to customer credit and vetting vendors — functions usually handled by finance or purchasing.

For marketing executives, risk management is a trial-and-error evolution. Has this agency produced good work previously? Will this vendor deliver on time? Experience has fine-tuned our instincts to a point where we intuitively assess risks based upon a combination of hundreds of deliberately and subconsciously collected data points.

Many executive committee members still view marketing as the last bastion of significant risk exposure. Everyone else from finance to operations, HR to IT employs robust risk-assessment tools and processes and highly effective ways to demonstrate the risk-adjusted outcomes of their key projects. They talk in terms of "net present value" of "future returns" associated with an investment made today. They link their recommendations to the bottom line and present their cases in such a way as to reassure not just the CEO, but also their peers, that they have carefully analyzed the financial, operational, organizational, and environmental risks and are proposing the optimal solution with the best likely outcome.

This process needs to be carried into the marketing measurement platform. Each proposed initiative or program should be evaluated not just on its total potential return, but on its risk-adjusted potential.

Here's an example: Let's say we're a retailer planning a holiday sale. We plan to run $1 million of TV advertising to drive traffic into stores during this one-day extravaganza. Using the reach and frequency data we get from our media department, combined with our assessment of the likely impact of the advertising copy, we estimate that about one million incremental customers will visit our stores on that day. If only 5% of them purchase at our average gross-margin per transaction of $20, we break even, right?

Unless, of course, it rains. In that case, our media will reach far more people watching TV inside, but far fewer will venture out to shop. Or maybe the weather will be fine, but one of our competitors will simultaneously announce a major sale event of their own featuring some attractive loss-leaders to entice traffic into their stores. Or maybe there will be some geopolitical news event that disturbs the normal economic optimism of our customers, causing them to cancel or postpone buying plans for a while.

Any or all of these things could happen. It only takes one to completely mess up the projected return on the $1 million investment in sale advertising.

Figure 4.5 — Risk Management Matrix

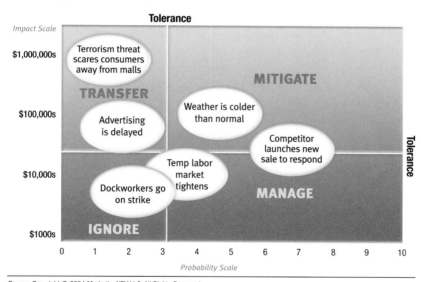

A strong measurement framework requires that each marketing initiative be thoroughly risk-assessed to identify all the bad things that could happen, the likelihood of them happening, and the potential impact if they did. The project forecast is then reduced accordingly. So if rain would cause a 50% drop in estimated store traffic and the weather forecast shows a 30% probability of rain in the area, our forecast for the event should be reduced by 15% (50% x 30%).

This structured risk-assessment approach will highlight investments that are more prone to external risk factors and modify their rosy expectations accordingly. In the end, high-risk, high-reward initiatives may be just what's required to achieve business goals, but wouldn't you rather know that's what you are approving, instead of finding it out later when high hopes are dashed?

The bibliography at the back of this book presents some excellent reading suggestions on risk-assessment and risk-management strategies. No marketing measurement framework is complete without the risk-management component in place.

CONCLUSION

Any discussion of dashboard development needs to begin with a thorough analysis of your ability to map and measure basic marketing performance. That means devotion to two critical concepts: funnel management and profit optimization.

While linear models linking awareness to perceptions to behaviors are rarely found to be accurate, they do provide a practical jumping-off point for beginning to ask the right questions. Mapping your funnel processes helps to clarify how marketing actions are intended to stimulate customer behaviors, which in turn create incremental cash flows. Exploding these processes out in detail helps create alignment while simultaneously drawing attention to some potentially powerful leading indicators for your dashboard.

The best dashboards are all about the infrastructure of an organization's measurement system. You can't see the inner workings, but without attention to their quality, the dashboard will be irrelevant from the start. We've found that many funnel and measurement efforts miss the boat by looking internally — focusing exclusively on financial results instead of buyer behavior. Focusing on buyers, even if it means developing entirely new ways to watch their behavior, leads you directly to the elements that produce profitability. And those are the areas worthy of priority consideration for your dashboard.

Sources

1. *MarketingNPV Journal*, vol. 1, issue 4.

2. Reibstein, Dave and Farris, Paul, The Wharton School of the University of Pennsylvania, 2005.

3. Tripodi, Joe, The Allstate Corporation.

4. ANA (Association of National Advertisers) and Forrester Research, "Marketing Accountability and Technology," 2004.

The Obvious Types of Metrics
(in Some Not-So-Obvious Forms)

When it comes to choosing metrics for a marketing dashboard, measurements are not only specific to industry, but to company, to division — right down to the specific department and the critical objectives at hand. As we've said, the marketing dashboard can be anything you want it to be as long as it shows the forward-looking information that benefits you most. In fact, the marketing dashboard should be tailored to meet the specific goals, objectives, and strategies of *your* company, its structure, and its unique culture.

Nevertheless, there are some categories of dashboard metrics that are appropriate in many circumstances. In this chapter and the next, we'll go over some of the more common ones. In Chapter 7, we'll take a look at some of the metrics you're likely to forget but shouldn't.

One note of terminology and philosophy as we begin our descriptions: Marketers show a tendency to use dashboard metrics that relate to revenue (topline sales) as opposed to profits (bottom line). This is a critical error that not only risks misleading decision makers about the effectiveness of marketing investments, but also perpetuates the cynicism with which other departments view marketing.

The potential to be misleading is relevant in that marketing costs must be allocated to the sales they generate *before* we determine the net incremental profits derived from the marketing investment. If we spend $5 million in marketing to generate $10 million in sales, fine. If the cost of goods sold (COGS, fully loaded with fixed cost allocations) is less than $4 million, we probably made money. But if the COGS is more than $4 million, we've delivered slightly better than breakeven on the investment and more likely lost money when taking into account the real or opportunity cost of capital.

Presenting marketing effectiveness metrics in revenue terms is seen as naive by the CFO and other members of the executive committee for very much the same reason as outlined above. Continuing to do so undermines the credibility of the marketing department, particularly when profits, contribution margins, or even gross margins can be approximated.

Why Revenue Metrics Can Be Dangerous

In our experience, there are several common rationalizations for using revenue metrics, including:

- limited data availability;
- an inability to accurately allocate costs to get from revenue to profit; and/or
- a belief that since others in the organization ultimately determine pricing and fixed and variable costs, marketing is primarily a topline-driving function that does not influence the bottom line.

To the first of these, we empathize. Many companies suffer from legacy sales reporting infrastructures where only the topline numbers are available or updated with a minimum of monthly frequency. If you're in one of those, we encourage you to use either the last month's or a 12-month rolling average net or gross margin percentage to apply to revenue. Finance can help you develop reasonable approximations to translate revenues to profits in your predictive metrics. You can always calibrate your approximations later when the actual numbers become available.

If you suffer from the second of these, an inability to allocate costs precisely, consider using "gross margins after marketing" (revenue less COGS less marketing expenses). Most companies know what their gross margins are by product line, and most CFOs are willing to acknowledge that incremental gross margins after marketing that exceed the overhead cost rate of the company are likely generating incremental profits. This is particularly true in companies in which the incremental sales derived from marketing activities are not necessitating capital investments in expanding production or distribution capacity. In short, engage finance in the conversation and collectively work to arrive at a best guess.

If you find yourself in the third group, you need to get your head out of the sand. The reality is that the mission of marketing is to generate incremental *profits*, not just revenue. If that means working with sales to find out how you need to change customer attitudes, needs, or perceptions to reduce the price elasticity for your products and services, do it. Without effective marketing to create value-added propositions for customers, sales may feel forced to continue to discount to make their goals, leading the entire organization into a slow death spiral — which, ironically, will start with cuts in the marketing budget.

If you *identified* with this third group, this should be a wake-up call that your real intentions for considering a dashboard are to *justify* your marketing expenditures, not really measure them for the purpose of improving. If that's the case, stop here and return this book. You're wasting your time. Your CEO and CFO will soon see your true motivation and won't buy into your dashboard anyway.

But if reading this is bringing you some personal enlightenment, re-read Chapter 3 and commit yourself to developing an effective strategy map. Then, draft a role of marketing contract to review with your CEO before you read on.

Having said all that, there are some times when using revenue metrics is highly appropriate. Usually those relate to measurements of share-of-customer spending or share-of-market metrics that relate to the total pie being pursued, not those attempting to measure the financial efficiency or effectiveness of the marketing investment.

In addition, be especially careful with metrics featuring ROI. If ROI is a function of the net change in profit divided by the investment required to achieve it, it can be manipulated by either reducing the investment or overstating the net profit change beyond that directly attributable to the marketing stimulus. Remember that the goal is to increase the net profit by as much as we can, as fast as we can, not just to improve the ROI. That's just a relative measure of efficiency in our approach, not overall effectiveness.

So, speaking of marketing efficiency metrics, let's start our review of common dashboard metrics here. Remember, most of these metrics are applicable to many industries. Try to extend our examples to your world to see if a given metric would be insightful for you.

Marketing Efficiency Metrics

Value/Volume Ratio

This is a basic calculation of marketing efficiency. It is the ratio of your estimated share of gross profits you're getting in your category compared to your share of the total volume sold in the category. For example, if you have a 19% share of volume by gallons of all the gas sold, but you only have a 14% share of total gross profits in the category, your value/volume ratio is 74% (14% divided by 19%). A ratio of less than 100% suggests you are buying your volume share through discounting and may need to course-correct by either reducing costs without reducing volume or by reducing the price elasticity of your customers through efforts to increase the perceived value of your product.

Marketing Cost Per Unit

Whatever your business, you sell "units" of something. It might be widgets or cases of widgets. It could be numbers of locomotive engines. Perhaps pounds of chemicals. Whatever your "units" are, you should be able to easily find out how many your company sells over a period of time. If you take the total marketing expense over that same period of time and divide by the number of units sold, you get a marketing cost per unit (MCPU). $1,000,000 in marketing expense divided by 250,000 units is $40 MCPU. Over time, you'd like to see the MCPU decline. You might also want to track your MCPU against your best estimates of your competitors.

Lag time is an important consideration if you're using MCPU. A dollar spent today on marketing may not influence a unit sale for several weeks or months. There is a strong argument that some of the money you're spending in marketing today is intended to create a long-term effect on unit sales that might not even show up in the current year. Regardless, you can likely discuss the lag time factors as a group (including finance) and arrive at an agreement on the expected timeframe of impact of the components of your marketing plan. When those expenses with long lag times are laid out on a calendar like the one in figure 5.1, they begin to overlap with short-term program expenses to create a total marketing cost in the current period. This provides the numerator for the calculation against the denominator of current period unit sales.

Over time, your accuracy at spreading marketing costs out over the proper period will increase, and hopefully your MCPU will improve as a reflection of increased efficiency.

FIGURE 5.1 — MARKETING COST PER UNIT

	P1	P2	P3	P4	P5	P6
Short-Term Programs	$2,435	$3,372	$2,889	$2,351	$3,253	$2,925
Amortized Long-Term Program A	$1,350	$350	$200	$100	$0	$0
Amortized Long-Term Program B	$0	$0	$2,150	$750	$400	$200
Total Marketing Investment	$3,785	$3,722	$5,239	$3,201	$3,653	$3,125
Total Units Sold (000s)	5738	5455	7539	5449	$5,823	$5,186
$ Marketing Per Unit	$0.66	$0.68	$0.69	$0.59	$0.63	$0.60

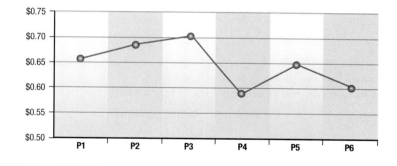

Marketing-Mix Productivity:

Marketing-mix models attempt to correlate investments in different communications media — broadcast, Internet, direct mail, print, outdoor — to actual sales volume. By using transactional data from all their points of sale, some companies can figure out the optimal mix for allocating marketing dollars. Unfortunately, most companies do their mix modeling on revenue, not profits. A dollar spent in one channel does not necessarily generate the same margin on a dollar in sales — so when discounting is done, sales may jump, but at the expense of profitability.

The scope of this book prohibits an in-depth discussion of mix models, but if you do have a mix model, consider reporting on the dashboard your overall contribution on total mix. If your modeling suggests you are getting $1.63 of contribution margin on each dollar of investment covered by the model, then your efficiency is 63%, before cost of capital. Showing how that efficiency improves over time will demonstrate good stewardship of company resources. Just be sure to keep the measurements consistent as market conditions (e.g., media rates, competitive activities, etc.) change.

Return on Important Initiatives

If there are one or more big-spending initiatives in your marketing plan like a substantial overhaul of your Web site, a new packaging launch, or just a big direct-marketing campaign, it may be appropriate to post the overall return for that project separately on your dashboard. If someone had to expend political capital to get the money to spend, you can underscore your commitment to getting the best return for the company's money by putting your progress right out where everyone can see it.

If the project has a target return that will take some time to achieve, consider reporting the work in progress, graphically comparing the present return to the goal in the form of a "thermometer" chart like the one in figure 5.2 below.

FIGURE 5.2 — PROFIT RETURN ON "PROJECT SPECTRE"

$4,000,000 Goal

Realized

23% $0

Program/Non-Program Ratio

This metric gives you the opportunity to look at the allocation of marketing resources to value-creating activities vs. overhead. Think about how charities are evaluated on the percentage of total funds raised that are distributed to the targeted recipients as opposed to salaries and overhead.

The higher the ratio, the more efficient the operation. The best charities are consistently in the 90%-plus range. What's your ratio? If the total marketing budget is $5 million, of which $4 million is allocated to specific program or campaign costs and $1 million to non-program costs, then your program/non-program ratio is 80%. There's your benchmark. Moving forward, you might set goals to increase that to 90% within two years.

It can be difficult to determine the line between value-creating activities and overhead, particularly when it comes to things like agency fees, payroll, staff development, or other issues. If this metric seems relevant to your situation, have a team develop a proposed delineation between program and non-program expenses and then try to apply it consistently over time. Consider breaking it into three categories instead of two:

- direct program resources;
- indirect program resources; and
- non-program resources.

Where you start from is less important than how well you progress toward your goal and keeping your definitions consistent.

Program/Payroll Ratio

This metric is a simpler form of the program/non-program ratio above. Take the total marketing budget and isolate the non-payroll-related expenses from the payroll dollars (fully loaded if applicable) to get a baseline of how the resources are allocated to customer-reaching activities vs. internal process management. Many marketing departments that do this for the first time are shocked at how high the percentage of total resources allocated to payroll are. It's not uncommon in some multidivisional B2B firms or others that don't do much advertising to find a 50/50 ratio.

Again, there's no particular benchmark for the right ratio beyond the target that you believe is reasonable given your marketing objectives. Importantly, everyone knows this metric can be easily manipulated by spending more money on existing advertising campaigns or shifting personnel from marketing into sales or operations. But if the metric is relevant to you, you'll find a way to define it in a manner that you can consistently apply in search of improvement in payroll leverage.

There might be 50 more metrics on this list based upon your company and industry. Understanding the purpose of marketing efficiency metrics is a good way to start the process of designing your own.

Customer Metrics

Here are a few thought-starters for how the customer might appear on the marketing dashboard.

Active Customer Counts

How many of your customers are "active" — consistently purchasing above some minimally acceptable level over time? This measure of customer-base vitality may tell you quite a bit about who is responding to your marketing activities and who is not. Consider looking at cohort groups of active customers by longevity if relevant. For example, what percentage of customers who first bought from you three years ago are still buying at least quarterly? What about those whose first purchase occurred only in the past 12 months? What is the difference between the two and why does it exist? How much are the groups purchasing and what is the product/service mix?

This metric might be even more telling when looked at from a profitability perspective than from a revenue view, but if vitality is really the question, revenue may suffice. If you don't have customer-specific transaction data but find this metric insightful, consider initiating either a panel study or tracking study of customers. Just keep the methodology consistent from period to period and the change over time will be more relevant than the absolute levels. And remember to keep the orientation towards the predictive. For example, let's say that we knew there were 400 plastic-stamping companies who purchased a chemical compound from us that helped keep the plastics malleable. At any given point in time, we know how many of them our company is doing business with and we have an action plan to increase that number. If we structure this correctly on the marketing dashboard, we will be able to monitor our results against our plan and see if we're projecting to close the gap on time and on budget.

FIGURE 5.3 — ACTIVE CUSTOMERS BY INCEPTION COHORT

	Q1	Q2	Q3	Q4
Inactive	12	15	17	18
Light Activity	21	27	25	28
Moderate Activity	16	14	15	17
Heavy Activity	9	12	13	16

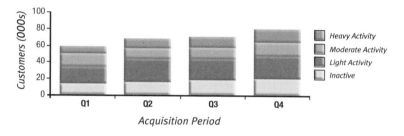

Segment Mobility

You can do frequency distributions of customers by *value* — the percentage or actual number of customers contributing different levels of profit or gross margin. Even if you can only define groups of customers in terms of low, moderate, and high profitability, these categories will give you more insight than topline revenue breaks.

You could also do frequency distribution of customers *across product lines*, meaning that you'll begin to track customers that are only buying one product during a time period vs. others who are buying two or more. Customer longevity is another option that gives you a broader picture of how well you're keeping customers in the fold.

Some companies develop combinations of value metrics that place customers into multidimensional segments that describe current and potential future value. RFM (recency, frequency, and monetary) analysis is the most common approach. Others use different combinations specific to their own circumstances. If you have a segmentation scheme that provides insights into future customer value (particularly in bottom-line terms), use it. Show how the customer base is migrating from one segment to another (hopefully more profitable) one. This is called segment mobility. See the example in figure 5.4.

FIGURE 5.4 — SEGMENT MOBILITY

Net Change in Segment Count vs. Forecast

From Segment: (To Segment:)	A	B	C	D	E
Segment A	1	4	-3	2	1
Segment B	0	4	12	4	-4
Segment C	0	1	0	1	2
Segment D	0	0	3	0	4
Segment E	0	0	0	5	-1

Some even prefer to focus on the velocity of segment mobility — the rate at which customers are migrating from one segment to another. All of these can become tremendously insightful, predictive metrics that forecast the health of the business.

The bottom line here is that frequency distributions are preferable to statements of average numbers because a simple frequency distribution graph implicitly tells you a lot more than an average ever can.

Share of Customer

Share of customer is your percentage of the total business that a customer does in your category. If the customer spends $3,600 a year on groceries and spends $1,200 a year in your grocery store, you have a 33% share of customer. This is another metric that works best in the form of a frequency distribution demonstrating mobility.

Share of customer is relatively easy to apply in categories in which the total annual purchase volume is more certain. For example, in retail gasoline, history has shown that the vast majority of consumers purchase between 1,000 and 1,200 gallons per year. So it's not that difficult to estimate share of customer if you know how much they purchased from you. But if you don't have transactional data on your customer's purchases or don't know what the likely total consumption volume is, you'll need to explore panel studies or survey techniques to develop estimates and then measure improvements over time using a consistent methodology.

Customer Loyalty, Repurchase, or Referral

There are lots of ways you can define "loyalty." Loyalty can be defined transactionally, meaning a person purchased from your company a certain number of times in a given period — a.k.a. the repurchase rate. Or loyalty can be defined emotionally, pointing to those customers who express a preference to do business with you in the future.

In the case of the former, you might choose to use dashboard metrics that portray the number or percentage of customers who purchased once, twice, or three-plus times in the last quarter vs. forecast and the prediction for the next few quarters. Or, if you are limited to survey data on attitudes and intentions, you might choose to highlight the percentage of respondents indicating top box or top two box answers to purchase intentions and look at:

■ how this most recent survey compares with prior surveys and the forecast response for this time period; and

■ how the expectation for the future may change.

Customer Experience Monitors

Here we get into the measurement of how consumers tell us they're happy or unhappy with what we're doing. They include the following:

■ **Satisfaction levels:** Satisfaction measures are always great candidates for a dashboard because they demonstrate information everyone wants to know. The trick, though, is to express this information predictively. Some companies are finding that one simple question is accurately predicting customer repurchase rates: "How likely are you to refer a friend or family member to do business with us in the next few months?" If that simplicity works for you, the answer to that one survey question can be a very predictive dashboard metric once calibrated.

■ **Quality perceptions:** Perceptions of quality are a terrific way to measure part of the customer experience. Understanding where you are meeting, exceeding, or falling short of expectations can help identify ways to improve the price/value relationship and decrease customer price elasticity.

■ **Order-cycle completion:** This is the time it takes from the minute you receive an order from a customer to the time that order leaves your factory or reaches your customer's hands — depending on how you define the cycle. Across industries, order-cycle completion tends to be highly correlated with customer satisfaction. It's a common dashboard metric because faster completed order times with accuracy can be easily calibrated over time as being predictive of reorders.

■ **Involvement/engagement levels:** Beyond just transactional behavior, profitable customers might have a tendency to be more involved with you or engaged in the relationship. This engagement can take many forms, including responses to customer surveys, providing testimonials, completing customer comment cards, or other alternatives. If you can establish that involvement among your customers and it's predictive of increasing customer profitability, reporting involvement and engagement levels on your dashboard is very appropriate.

■ **Repurchase intentions:** Survey-driven findings indicate how likely customers are to repurchase and how much they'll spend when they do. It is important to know that these findings contain margins of error because there is a tendency for the consumer to either overstate or understate their intentions. However, if you survey consistently with the right methodology over time and are able to track the stated intention to the subsequent actual behavior, you can develop a correction factor that you can apply to a stated intention. That will give you a fairly accurate, highly predictive view of how much you're likely to sell to that customer or segment of customers in the future.

■ **Compliments/complaints:** This is a test for your inbound channels — call centers, Web sites, etc. The nature, frequency, and magnitude of compliments or complaints are worth tracking on an ongoing basis as long as you can add some predictive value to the measurement.

■ **Resolution turnaround times:** When you have a problem, how fast do you fix it? If your company is in a turnaround situation in which you know you have customer issues that need repair, this is a worthy subject to measure.

No company is going to find all of these measures appropriate. But depending upon where you are in organizational sophistication and capability, some of these may be effective metrics for your dashboard. The whole area of customer experience monitors is often overlooked as dashboard metrics because of concerns that self-reported responses are methodologically suspect. But if you spend the time to develop a good methodology and you apply it consistently, the error factor normalizes over time. In other words, you see the same type and magnitude of error in each iteration of the survey, thereby eliminating the error and leaving only the real trend.

For example, if your Uncle Ernie consistently overestimates the number of loud teenage kids on his block by 5% to 10%, you can rely on his estimates in the future by subtracting 5% to 10% from whatever number he gives you. Likewise, if you find the error rate in self-reported purchase activity among customers is consistent over time, you can calibrate it to actual purchase activity with a high degree of confidence. You can use it to be very predictive with respect to future sales.

Return on Customer^SM

Your customers are assets. Properly nurtured, they'll improve in profitability over time as they look to you to meet more of their needs. They'll hopefully purchase from you more efficiently and with less price elasticity.

You spend a certain amount of money to attract, retain, and nurture these customers. They in turn not only buy from you, but also refer others to do the same. In some industries, the lifetime value of these customer relationships can be ascertained within reason. When that lifetime value per customer is multiplied by the number of customers, you get a total value of the customer base. The investment you make in securing and defending those customers can then be compared to the change in the value of the base to get a "Return on Customer." For example, if you spent $25 million last year and achieved a net change in customer value of $50 million, your Return on Customer would be 100%.

This is an emerging thought process in gauging asset value. It has many potential challenges for most businesses. But if your company is oriented toward customer value creation, it might be a direction worthy of consideration for your dashboard with two caveats: First, as with most ROI metrics, be careful not to focus on the percentage return. It can be manipulated by reducing spend or claiming growth associated with marketing that would have occurred without the marketing stimulus. Second, believing that any single all-encompassing metric can consistently and accurately gauge marketing effectiveness is wishful thinking at best.

Brand management is a crucial aspect of marketing effectiveness and we'll dedicate ourselves to brand scorecard metrics in Chapter 6. In Chapter 7, we'll explore some less traditional dashboard metrics that may nevertheless be highly relevant for you.

CONCLUSION

Marketing efficiency metrics are very common starting places for marketing dashboards. Likewise, most dashboards include some perspective on customer profitability evolution. We've presented some examples of effective metrics in these categories as thought-starters to help you identify relevant metrics for your industry and company. We also underscored the importance of incorporating customer experience metrics as the voice of the customer on your dashboard.

SOURCES

Return on Customer is a registered service mark of Peppers and Rogers Group, a division of Carlson Marketing Group, Inc.

Putting the Brand on the Dashboard: Building a Brand Scorecard within Your Dashboard

The marketing dashboard is intended to track both the inputs — the marketing activities being undertaken — and the outputs — the financial results generated. If you've followed closely so far, you can see that leaves the possibility of a gap in the middle, which is the asset that's being created beyond the P&L in the mind of the customer.

Measuring the long-term value of marketing in creating customer preference and loyalty for your brand(s) is critically important in determining the return from the investment. Depending upon your industry or category, 50%, 60%, 70%, or more of your marketing expenditures may be in support of programs and initiatives that cannot be shown to have short-term effects on incremental profits, but *can* be shown to improve the health of the brand in the marketplace. But if this "brand health" isn't something we can easily translate into forecast profits this year, we need to treat it as an asset — something that generates positive returns over a longer period of time.

This is where a brand scorecard comes in. The brand scorecard tracks the health of the brand in the minds of the customers. Whereas the marketing dashboard tends to look at things more from the company's point of view — "What investments are made in programs and initiatives and what I should expect to get out in terms of customer behavior?" — the brand scorecard asks, "What do our major constituencies of interest think and feel about our brand and how well is our brand supporting our desired value propositions?"[1]

In a comprehensive marketing dashboard, the brand scorecard stands somewhere in the middle between the inputs and the outputs.

Let's take a look at what the critical elements of a brand scorecard are, how many constituencies it should reflect, and why it deserves to be treated specially within the dashboard.

The Problem with Brand Scorecards Today

There aren't enough of them. That's the problem with brand score-cards today.

If you ask 100 companies to show you their brand scorecard (and we have), 20 will look at you quizzically, another 20 will show you elaborate consumer surveys of brand attribute ratings, and the remaining 60 will pull out a research summary of the latest scores on the classic "hierarchy of effects" waterfall:

- 74% of consumers are aware of the brand on an unaided basis
  - ❖ 61% indicate an overall favorable impression of the brand
    - ▲ 47% indicate a willingness to try the product

… and so on.

The problem with this typical waterfall is that it never actually connects awareness or preferences to value creation, and as such is seen by the CFO and the rest of the finance department as "marketing mumbo jumbo" used to justify spending money.

Awareness is a not an achievement unto itself. Each of us is personally aware of a great many companies that we know nothing about. We don't know what they make or do, and even if we do, we have no clue as to why we might want to buy their product or service. We may have an awareness of these companies, but no *salience* to that awareness that places it into a proper context for us.

Salience itself may have multiple levels. I may know IBM makes computers, but I may not know they make the kind of Web servers I need for my company. Or maybe I know they make Web servers, but I think they offer solutions only in the high-performance/high-priced end of the market.

Preference also has many potential dimensions and degrees. I may prefer to drive a Jaguar, but have no realistic hope of ever being able to afford one. I might thereby "prefer" the Hyundai to the Kia, but do I really "prefer" the Hyundai?

The aforementioned example indicates how brand preference is of little value absent the proper context. My preference for a given brand should be measured within the context of those that are physically available to me and within my affordability zone. Preference should also be measured in a temporal context — relative to the point in time when I am most likely to translate my attitudes into behavior and buy.

When it comes to willingness to try the brand, the wheels really come off. Just because I'm willing to try it doesn't mean I ever actually will. Maybe if I get a coupon for 50% off I'll consider it, but if it's not available where I normally buy, my willingness is strictly theoretical.

Purchase intentions are only valid when the prospective customer has the appropriate salient awareness, knows where to buy the product, understands what the tradeoffs are within the competitive set, and has the money and desire to act. Only then are the intentions appropriately qualified.

There's little doubt that salient awareness, contextual preference, and qualified purchase intentions *can* be valuable indicators of the potential economic value of the brand. But until they are unlocked and flowing freely from the minds and hearts of the customers to their wallets and into our company treasury, we must find a way to measure them for what they are: Assets. Good intentions. Accumulated goodwill toward the brand that has not yet translated into a financial outcome.

A brand is a reservoir of future cash flows not yet realized.

— Tim Ambler, Senior Fellow, London Business School[2]

The role of the brand scorecard within the marketing dashboard is to reflect the evolution of these brand assets and continually gauge the potential value of the demand they represent. For this unique reason, we recommend setting up the brand scorecard as a separate-but-linked portion of the overall marketing dashboard. Doing so helps to highlight both the input/output importance of the dashboard and the asset-nurturing insights of the brand scorecard.

To begin, let's look at the potential cornerstones of any consumer/customer brand scorecard.

Four Key Attributes for the Brand Scorecard

Every company and possibly every brand will have its own view of the most crucial components of the customer's brand decision process. Some choose to use syndicated approaches to brand measurement like Young & Rubicam's BrandAsset® Valuator or Millward Brown's Brand Tracker. Others have developed an exhaustive battery of brand attributes they measure through elaborate tracking studies. Regardless of the approach you are using (or if you're just starting out), the key consideration is to find the elements that are most predictive of the future behavior of prospects and customers.

In general, there are four dimensions of brand measurement that tend to bind the customer to the brand:

- the functional performance of the underlying product or service;
- the convenience and ease of accessing the product or service;
- the personality of the brand (a.k.a. "the one for me"); and
- the pricing and value component.

The functional dimension seeks to measure the customer's (or prospect's) perceptions of the more tangible aspects of their brand experience. Is the product of sufficient quality? Does it work as promised? Is it more durable, more flexible, more efficient, more yellow, more professional, more appropriate to the intended task than perceived substitutes? Each brand is intended to deliver a combination of functional benefits to the user, be it a toothpaste, financial services, or silicone polymers. The brand scorecard should reflect how well these functional elements are perceived by the experience of regular customers vs. the newly acquired customers and how they compare to the perceptions of the imminent prospects vs. those in the target audience at large.

Each brand also has, as part of its fundamental equity structure, perceptions and knowledge about where to buy the product or try the service. Can I get it at my local mass merchant store? Do I buy it on the Web? Will an agent come to my home? The degree to which the prospects are aware of how they would acquire or access the brand

and their perceptions of the acceptability of that avenue are important components of the brand asset value. Likewise, the perspectives of the current customers of the ease of access through the present distribution channels provide an important opportunity to validate or question the current business process.

Brand personality is very important in many categories. As marketers, we all understand how one soft drink might have a different "personality" than another. For many years now, marketing researchers have used personification exercises to get consumers to describe a product as male/female, young/old, progressive/conservative, outgoing/shy. Corporate brands also tend to have key personality traits like "reliable," "trustworthy," "innovative," etc. If you can establish that certain personality profiles, when attached to your brand, increase the likeliness of prospects becoming customers and customers buying more, then those critical elements should be on your brand scorecard.

Last, but certainly not least, brands often exist for one primary purpose — to differentiate competitive offerings and prevent commoditization of the market. Brands are used to imbue certain companies or products with a premium value perception that commands a premium price. In other categories, brands are used to capture the consumer gratitude for being the lowest price provider. In either extreme, or at any point in the middle of that spectrum, every brand has a price/value component to it that is either the bedrock of its success or a competitive requirement to compete effectively. This "absolute price" perception is often worthy of tracking on the brand scorecard.

The second dimension of pricing is the "relative price" — a measure of the extent to which prospects and customers perceive that your brand offers good "value for the money." Continuously gauging the relative price perceptions is an effective way to quickly identify opportunities for market or margin share increases.

The combination of functional, accessibility, personality, and value attributes of the brand often provide a well-rounded picture of how well the brand asset is growing and how much untapped cash flow is waiting to be unlocked.

But you have to do the spade work to understand the links between brand equities and financial success in your category. What is often thought to cause people to purchase — Brand A seems to do the job better than Brand B — quickly goes out the window when the choice is guided by, "I really can't be bothered to think about it. Brand A is available now, and Brand B isn't." If this is common in your category, then some kind of distribution weight or availability of the product can be a more important scorecard metric than one that measures the degree to which the customers believe your brand has a special functional characteristic or has a personality "like me."

Sometimes it's sufficient to have your brand just penetrate the competitive set and then out-execute the competition on distribution or packaging. Knowing what *really* drives your brand category is critical to selecting the scorecard metrics that will be both most diagnostic and most predictive of future success.

This generic framework can be applied across different categories, although the weight of the individual components may actually vary dramatically.

Timing Your Measurements

Another important thing to consider is that brand perceptions aren't static — consumer loyalties can last over a lifetime or end in a few short days. And that often runs counter to a company's own brand perception, which can remain pointlessly unchanged. Most companies, even many with huge research budgets, don't carefully monitor the clarity, or lack of clarity, their brand has with customers and prospects at any given point in time. A brand value proposition that made a lot of sense under one set of industry circumstances may degrade to irrelevance and become a commodity position if it stays too long in one place.

Most often, brand attributes are monitored in large-scale tracking studies conducted in "waves" three, six, or 12 months apart. If your category evolves faster than the frequency of your tracking studies, these periodic reads may provide irrelevantly historical information and present a picture that bears little resemblance to today's reality

— especially when you consider that it often takes four to six weeks from the end of survey fielding until the report gets on your desk.

Many organizations are today migrating towards "continuous" brand tracking, with smaller samples fielded each week or each month that are then read in the aggregate over a rolling six, eight, or 12 weeks. While a bit more expensive, this approach can provide much more timely insights into the shifts of the marketplace, not to mention the potential to measure the impacts of marketing stimulus programs on brand attributes with greater reliability.

The bottom line is you need to clearly know what your brand is and what it means to the target customer. If you don't, you are prone to serious over- or underestimations of your brand strength. One such failure was Reebok's attempt to market a Reebok brand of water. Reebok thought that Reebok stood for health. In reality, it stood for running shoes. Why would anyone want to drink water out a shoe?

Without an effective brand scorecard, you might not have an accurate picture of where your brand stands or where it's headed. With one, you have no excuses not to.

IN SEARCH OF A RELIABLE MEASURE OF BRAND EQUITY

By Jonathan Knowles, Senior Strategist, Wolff Olins

Accountability is the new black for marketers. According to a survey taken earlier this year by the Association of National Advertisers (ANA) of 1,000 marketing executives, 66% ranked the accountability of marketing as their number-one concern. A similar study by the CMO Council revealed that 80% of respondents were "dissatisfied" with their ability to measure ROI.

While the desire of marketers to demonstrate that they are allocating marketing investments as efficiently as possible is admirable, they are doing themselves a disservice with their current obsession with ROI. By interpreting marketing accountability solely in terms of a metric of short-term payback, marketers are reinforcing the impression of marketing as a merely tactical discipline.

The bigger question — and the one that will earn marketers a seat at the boardroom table in a way that no amount of ROI measurement can — is whether brands truly are assets that enable the business to generate superior returns over time.

The first point for marketers to recognize is that, to qualify as an "asset" in financial terms, a brand needs to be measured in terms of its ability to generate future cash flow.

The second point is even more important: Value can only be created by changes in customer behavior. Changes in customer attitudes are nice, but in and of themselves they do not generate cash flow.

This means that many of the traditional metrics favored by marketers — awareness, familiarity, and quality — are no longer suitable as measures of brand equity. They still do a good job of measuring the scale of a brand's market presence and the likelihood that the brand will make it into a given customer's consideration set. However, they do a poor job of explaining the final purchase decision, and therefore do not provide a reliable measure of the brand's ability to generate cash flow.

The reason for this is that Total Quality Management (TQM) has driven genuinely bad products and services out of the market. Those that remain are all of satisfactory quality, meaning that the customer now faces a bewildering array of good alternatives. In response to this, the basis for the final purchase decision has expanded from simply, "What will you do for me?" to, "What will you do for me — and mean to me?"

So the third point is that brand equity needs to be measured in a way that captures the source and scale of this emotional augmentation that the brand provides to the underlying functionality of the product or service. Only such a definition of brand equity will identify the extent of the customer utility that the brand has created.

There are two promising candidates for how this equity can be measured:

- The first type of approach measures equity in terms of "outcomes," such as the extent to which customers are prepared to stake their personal or professional reputation behind a brand by recommending it to others or the price premium they are prepared to pay.
- The second type of approach measures equity in terms of the scale and nature of the utility that the brand delivers to customers.

One of the best known examples of the "outcome" type of approach is the work of Fred Reichheld, the author of *The Loyalty Effect* (1996) and *Loyalty Rules* (2001). His simple premise is that "willingness to recommend to a friend" is the single most reliable measure of brand equity. Specifically, your "net promoter" score (the number of people willing to recommend your brand minus those who are not willing to do so) provides an accurate predictor of your company's growth prospects.

In similar vein are approaches that stress "willingness to pay a price premium" as the truest test of the existence of brand equity. And the advantage of these approaches is that they provide a direct input into a valuation model like the "revenue premium" methodology advocated by Professor Don Lehmann of Columbia University.

The limitation of "outcome" approaches is that, while they may accurately quantify how much brand equity you enjoy, they provide limited insight into what creates this equity.

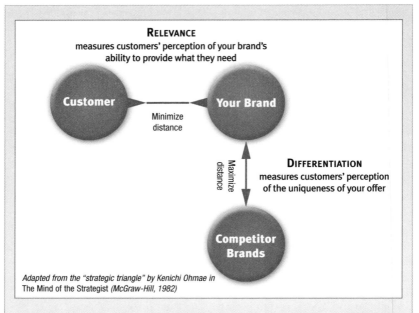

RELEVANCE
measures customers' perception of your brand's
ability to provide what they need

Customer

Your Brand

Minimize
distance

Maximize
distance

DIFFERENTIATION
measures customers' perception
of the uniqueness of your offer

Competitor
Brands

Adapted from the "strategic triangle" by Kenichi Ohmae in
The Mind of the Strategist *(McGraw-Hill, 1982)*

The second type of approach tries to quantify the extent of brand equity that a brand enjoys by measuring the degree of "relevant differentiation" provided (although most do not explicitly use this term). Relevant differentiation is an important metric because it measures the success of marketing in terms of the extent to which two goals have been achieved — maximization of the perceived fit between your brand and your customer's needs, and maximization of the perceived differentiation of your brand vs. its competitors. A high relevant differentiation score provides insight into why a certain brand is perceived to be uniquely capable of meeting customer needs.

Following are profiles of a number of well-established brand equity models that seek to identify the scale and sources of brand equity.

Equity Engine^SM

Equity Engine^SM, developed by Research International, is one of the most elegantly parsimonious models of brand equity. Essentially, it expresses brand equity as a combination of the functional benefits delivered by the brand (perform-ance) and the emotional benefits (affinity). Underlying each of these macro constructs is a further layer of analysis that expresses performance as a function of product and service attributes, and affinity as a function of the brand identification (the closeness customers feel to the brand), approval (the status the brand enjoys among a wider social context of family, friends, and colleagues), and authority (the reputation of the brand).

Equity Engine[SM] incorporates a form of conjoint methodology that establishes the price premium that a brand's equity will support while still maintaining a "good value for money" rating from customers.

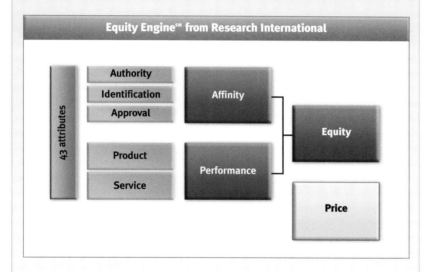

Equity*Builder

Equity*Builder, the methodology developed by the Ipsos Group, is more uniquely focused on establishing the emotional component of brand equity. Importantly, it situates a brand's attitudinal equity (measured in terms of differentiation, relevance, popularity, quality, and familiarity) in the context of the degree of customer involvement with the category in question.

Similar to Equity Engine[SM], Equity*Builder also explicitly addresses how brand equity translates into perceived value and price.

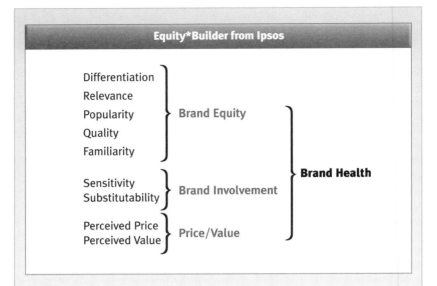

BrandAsset® Valuator

The BrandAsset® Valuator, developed by Young & Rubicam, is noteworthy in that it eschews the category-specific approach taken by other brand equity methodologies and seeks to establish a pure measure of brand equity independent of category context. All 2,500 brands in its U.S. survey are rated on the same 48 attributes and four macro constructs of differentiation, relevance, esteem, and knowledge (curiously similar to the Ipsos approach, which it pre-dates).

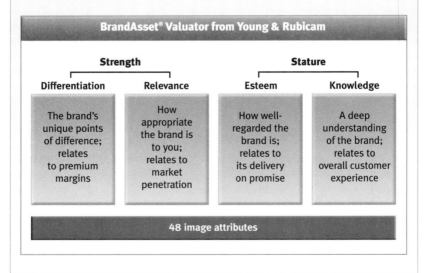

The constructs of differentiation and relevance are then combined into a single metric of brand strength that, through Young & Rubicam's collaboration with the financial consultancy Stern Stewart, has been shown to provide a powerful explanation of superior market value. The constructs of esteem and relevance are combined to form brand stature that, interestingly, is correlated to current market share but not potential for growth.

Kevin Lane Keller's Model

Although not available as a commercial methodology, Kevin Lane Keller's brand equity model is worthy of mention because of his authority within the brand equity measurement arena. (He is professor of marketing at the Tuck School of Business at Dartmouth and recently co-authored the 12th edition of *Marketing Management* with Philip Kotler.)

Kevin Lane Keller mirrors the Equity Engine℠ approach by seeing the brand as a blend of the rational and the emotional, measured in terms of performance characteristics and imagery. Customers' relationship to a brand can be plotted in terms of their altitude on the pyramid of engagement and their relative bias towards a rationally dominant or emotionally dominant relationship.

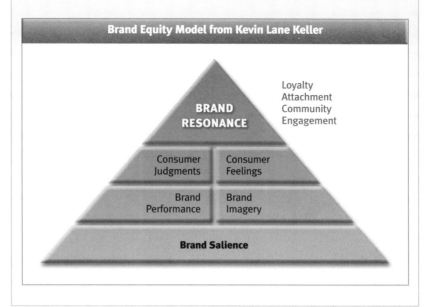

Brand Equity Model from Kevin Lane Keller

BrandDynamics™

The notion of a pyramid of engagement is echoed in the BrandDynamics™ methodology developed by Millward Brown. This approach characterizes the relationship that a customer has with a brand into one of five stages: presence, relevance, performance, advantage, and bonding. "Presence" customers have only a basic awareness of the brand, while "bonded" customers are intensely loyal, at least in their attitudes. The underlying premise is that the lifetime value of customers increases the higher up they are in the pyramid.

All of the aforementioned approaches suffer from the fact that they are attitudinal in nature and have yet to establish the definitive relationship between measures of attitudinal engagement/loyalty and observed behavior.

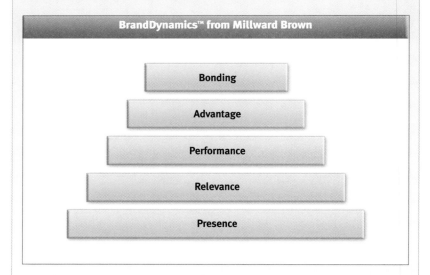

Winning Brands™

Winning Brands™ is the methodology developed by ACNielsen. In contrast to the attitudinal approach to brand equity measurement embodied in the other approaches described, Winning Brands begins from a behavioral observation of brand equity. Brand equity is measured in terms of a customer's frequency of purchase and the price premium paid. Once favorable behavior is observed, the methodology seeks to analyze the attitudinal characteristics of those customers.

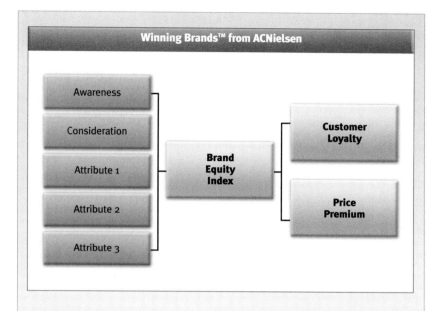

The strategic component of brand development involves the creation and nurturing of a long-lived corporate asset. Of potentially greater importance than a credible ROI model for marketers is the development of a robust methodology for defining and measuring brand equity in a way that meets the financial requirement for an asset, namely that it represents a source of incremental cash flow over time. This means that the focus needs to be on the metrics that capture and explain customer behavior, not simply customer attitudes.

Originally appeared in MarketingNPV Journal, *vol. 2, issue 3, pages 16-19.*

Brand Value vs. Brand Valuation

To be a useful tool for organizational planning and resource allocation, the brand scorecard needs to go beyond attribute ratings and incorporate a second key measurement — an understanding of brand value.

There's a difference between "brand value" and "brand valuation." Brand value is the strategic and financial value of the brand to your company today. Brand valuation is a financial exercise intended to put a price on the brand over and above the discounted future cash flows. The difference can be subtle. Tim Ambler of the London Business School uses this metaphor to describe the two: "Since I live in my house and plan to do so for some time, its *value* to me is the shelter and comfort I derive from it. When I'm prepared to consider selling it, I'll be interested in the valuation." Brands work much the same way.

Let's look first at brand value.

Brands create value for companies in several ways:

- They create customer loyalty, resulting in a lower cost of customer reacquisition and greater likelihood of future sales from existing customers.
- They lower the perception of risk the company presents to the financial marketplace, resulting in lower borrowing or financing costs.
- They establish negotiating leverage with suppliers and vendors who seek to be associated with them.
- They establish the perception of continuity of cash flows into the future amongst investors, thereby increasing the multiple over the company book value that investors are willing to pay for stock.

If these dimensions of brand value are relevant ways for you to gauge the potential return you will create by investing in brand development activities, then they should be reflected on your brand scorecard. You may choose to reflect it in competitive comparisons of expected customer lifetime value, perceptions of company "quality" amongst investors and analysts (either through syndicated methods like CoreBrand® or through proprietary research among targeted analysts), an index of company borrowing costs that isolates brand contributions from other marketplace and company variables, or a survey of brand influence within the vendor community.

The most common measure of brand value is one of the difference between market capitalization and either "book value" — the value of the company's total balance sheet assets — or the net present value of expected future cash flows. Unfortunately, it's not often reasonable to assume that the difference is mostly attributable to brand value. Channel dominance, patents and technical advantages, sales force effectiveness, and other non-brand elements can be responsible for a big portion of the "intangible" value of the company.

Nevertheless, if your category is one in which investments in brand development are less directly justifiable in terms of customer financial behavior in the near term, you may need to incorporate some element of brand value in your analysis. The best advice we can offer is to sit down with your CFO and discuss the ways you might agree on measuring the brand asset. Typically those fall into two classes. The first is made up of top-down models that seek to explain valuation in terms of the lift in share price that the brand gives you over and above what the company would trade at without a brand. The second approach comes at it from the bottom up. Often called the "economic use" approach, this is an attempt to measure how much incremental cash flow the brand provides over and above what you would get with a "generic" product. The two are philosophically very well aligned. One comes from the macro and hopes to explain the micro, and the other hopes to aggregate the micro to explain superior valuation for the company.

"Brand valuation," on the other hand, may be relevant to you if your portfolio of brands includes some acquired from other companies, or if you anticipate selling one or more brands at some point in the not-too-distant future.

Accounting regulations in the United States and many other countries require companies to keep close tabs on the "goodwill" assets they carry on their balance sheets from past acquisitions. If the CFO has reason to believe that any acquired brand is no longer worth its carrying value on the balance sheet, she must take a write-down against earnings on the P&L to revise the estimate of value in a process called "asset impairment."

As a result, companies with acquired brands often need to continually monitor the value of those brands on their brand scorecard to prevent any sudden surprises in earnings.

Similarly, if your company anticipates selling itself in the whole or just selling one or more brands in its portfolio, you may want to begin tracking brand valuation over the period leading up to the sale to understand which potential investments help increase the valuation and which might actually detract from it. The brand score-card can be useful in this regard, too.

If you're not marketing acquired brands or planning on selling your own, the remaining reasons to do brand valuation are mostly tax-related or technical/financial and likely not important for a brand scorecard.

DON'T WASTE TIME WITH BRAND VALUATION

By David Haigh, Founder and CEO, Brand Finance, and Jonathan Knowles, Senior Strategist, Wolff Olins

There is widespread acceptance among senior management that strong brands represent significant assets of a business. With high levels of competition and excess capacity in virtually every industry, strong brands enable companies to differentiate themselves and to provide a basis for ongoing customer loyalty.

At the same time, there is a widespread but erroneous assumption that brands need to be valued. The publication of tables of brand values in magazines such as *BusinessWeek*, *Forbes*, and a number of marketing publications has raised the profile of brand valuation but unfortunately has done so without clarifying its purpose.

It is an obvious point but one that bears repeating — the mere act of valuing an asset, whether financial, tangible, or intangible, does nothing to improve its quality. Most companies do not need an answer to the question "What is the value of my brand?" except for the specific purpose of accounting for goodwill after an acquisition. Rather they need an answer to the question "How — and by how much — does my brand contribute to the overall success of my business?" It is this insight into the sources of customer value and the economic cost of delivering that value that will enable them to run more successful businesses. Brand value on its own provides nothing more than bragging rights at corporate cocktail parties.

In light of this, we suggest that companies should begin from the position that they do not need to value their brand(s) unless they have compelling answers to the following:

- What commercial objective will be served by a brand valuation?
- What is the asset we will be measuring if we do a brand valuation?

What Commercial Objective Will Be Served by a Brand Valuation?

In our experience, there are three basic reasons why a brand valuation may be justified:

1. It is required for accounting purposes.
2. It will inform the terms of a prospective transaction.
3. It will enhance our management of the brand.

Accounting purposes

Since March 31, 2004, gone are the significant differences that previously had separated international and U.S. rules on accounting for business acquisitions. Both U.S. and international rules (respectively Financial Accounting Standard 141 in the United States and International Financial Reporting Standard 3 from the International Accounting Standard Board) require that all identifiable intangible assets of the acquired business be recorded at fair value. This ends the previous practice of treating the excess of the purchase price over the net tangible assets acquired as a single goodwill figure.

Now there is a requirement that this single goodwill figure will be broken down into a number of specific intangible assets, leaving only a small residual amount of unidentified goodwill. The types of intangible assets that are now to be expressly recognized include technology-based assets, such as patents; contract-based assets, such as leases and licensing agreements; artistic assets, such as plays and films; customer-based assets, such as customer lists; and marketing-related assets, such as trademarks and brands.

If you acquired a number of brands as a result of an acquisition, U.S. and international rules now require you to report a value for these brands on your balance sheet. A recent example is the acquisition of the Miller Brewing Co. by South African Breweries. The Miller brands represent $4.5 billion of the $6.5 billion of intangible assets that appear on the SAB Miller balance sheet for 2003.

Transactional purposes

The second circumstance in which a brand valuation may be justified is to inform the terms of a prospective transaction. The transaction may be internal or external.

The two most common types of internal transactions involving brands are securitization or tax planning. Securitization involves raising funds against the security of future revenues, such as the $55 million that David Bowie raised in 1997. The "Bowie bonds" were backed by the future royalties anticipated on his pre-1990 records. Despite a lot of discussion, brands have rarely been used as the collateral in asset-backed securities.

Brand-based tax planning is, by contrast, a relatively common practice. Companies transfer the ownership of their brand and other intellectual property assets to a central holding company. The central IP holding company then charges a royalty for the use of these assets to the operating companies, enabling a portion of the profits of these operating companies to be shielded from local taxes. Obviously, the fiscal authorities require demonstration of the value of the brand asset that provides the basis for these royalty payments.

External transactions involving brands usually take the form of acquisitions of branded companies or of licensing of brands from third parties. In each case, commercial due diligence is required to verify the economic value of the asset being acquired or licensed and to inform the discussion over the deal terms. In the case of acquisitions, the knowledge that accounting rules now require allocation of the purchase price between the different types of assets acquired has heightened the significance of the preacquisition due diligence process.

Management of the brand

The third commercial purpose that can be served by a brand valuation is the one that offers both the most opportunity for value enhancement and the greatest danger of wasted effort and expense.

In contrast to the technical and financial applications of brand valuation outlined here, in this case, the purpose of the valuation is purely to improve marketing's effectiveness. In theory its goal is to measure the extent to which brands enhance the underlying business performance and valuation of the company. In practice, the valuation model often gets subverted and used for defending marketing budgets.

The second major source of danger is that a brand valuation for marketing purposes requires greater thought about the nature of the asset being valued. Brand valuations for technical and financial purposes generally focus on a narrow definition of brand as the bundle of legally enforceable intellectual property rights that the brand owner has established. These center on the trademark itself but frequently also encompass the associated goodwill that the brand enjoys among its customers.

The specific details of the extent of the assets covered in the acquisition of a branded company were powerfully illustrated by Volkswagen's acquisition of Rolls Royce Motors for $667 million in 1988. The acquisition included all of the physical assets of the production of Rolls Royce and Bentley automobiles. But BMW, in a separate transaction, acquired the rights to use the Rolls Royce trademark in automobiles for $62 million.

Where a brand valuation is being contemplated for marketing purposes, considerable emphasis should be placed on determining the nature of the asset being valued.

What Is the Asset We Will Be Measuring If We Do a Brand Valuation?

In our experience there are three distinct definitions of the asset, all of which are sometimes referred to as the brand.

A logo and associated visual elements. This is the most specific definition of brand, focusing on the legally protectable, visual, and verbal elements that are used to differentiate one company's products and services from another's and to stimulate demand for those products and services. The main legal elements covered by this definition are trade names, trademarks, and trade symbols.

However, in order to add value, trademarks and trade symbols need to carry "associated goodwill" in the minds of customers based on the experience or reputation of high-quality products and good service.

A valuation based on this definition of brand is more properly called a trademark valuation.

A larger bundle of trademark and associated intellectual property rights. Under this definition, "brand" is extended to encompass a larger bundle of intellectual property rights such as domain names, product design rights, trade dress, packaging, copyrights in associated colors, smells, sounds, descriptors, logotypes, advertising visuals, and written copy.

Some commentators have interpreted the intellectual property rights included in the definition of brand to encompass tangible as well as intangible property rights (for example, to include the recipe and production process in the case of Guinness). This more holistic view is consistent with the opinion that brand is a much broader and deeper experience than the logo and associated visual elements.

This is the definition of brand that is generally intended when talking about a brand valuation in a marketing context.

A holistic company or organizational brand. The debate as to which intellectual property rights should be incorporated into the definition of "brand" often leads to the view that brand refers to the whole organization within which the specific logo and associated visual elements plus the larger bundle of "visual and marketing intangibles" and the "associated goodwill" are deployed.

A combination of all these legal rights, together with the culture, people, and programs of an organization, all provide a basis for differentiation and value creation by that organization. Taken as a whole, they represent a specific value proposition and foundation for strong customer, supplier, and staff relationships. This definition of brand serves as the basis for a branded business valuation. This broader perspective on the business is of significant value to those with strategic planning responsibilities. It illuminates the principal value drivers of the business and identifies how brand perceptions and preferences affect consumer purchase behavior and enrich staff and supplier relationships. As such, it makes a substantive contribution to understanding the sources and scale of a company's competitive position. It quantifies the size of the asset that the brand represents and — perhaps more important — identifies ways in which the value can be enhanced.

Going for Substance over Style

It comes as a surprise to many business professionals that the majority of brand valuations are performed for purposes other than marketing. But, as we have outlined here, there is a demonstrated commercial purpose for brand valuation in the context of accounting, tax planning, and commercial due diligence. Brand valuation for marketing purposes suffers from some muddled thinking.

Most senior marketers embrace the idea of value-based brand strategy and see brand valuation as a means to this end (and a basis for a compelling presentation to the C-suite). We applaud this goal but still advise caution before valuable resources are committed to a brand-valuation exercise. The process of valuing intangible assets such as human capital or brands is fraught with issues of definition, methodology, and measurement, with the result that the exercise frequently fails to deliver the expected benefits. For this reason, we recommend that significant thought be given to the interrelated issues of the commercial goal that will be supported by the brand valuation and the definition of "brand" to be used in the valuation.

Doing so will avoid some of the most frequent issues that arise due to the need to reconcile the economic, management reporting, and accounting perspectives on brand. It will also clarify whether the goal of value-based brand strategy and management might not be better served by devoting resources to better understanding the sources of customer value and the relative strength of a brand's equity rather than to brand valuation.

Originally appeared in MarketingNPV Journal, *vol. 1, issue 6, pages 17-19.*

Measuring All the Relevant Constituencies

As you might tell from the previous discussion of brand value and valuation, when we set up a brand scorecard we need to monitor the health of the brand with at least four key audiences: customers, employees, relevant society at large, and investors. Your circumstances might dictate including additional constituencies such as channel partners, agents, regulators, etc.

A good scorecard should cover employee perspectives on the brand, as well as customers and prospects. It's particularly important in service and retail industries, as associates are increasingly asked to play ambassadorial roles. Many companies consider the entire associate population to be "brand managers" as they define the ultimate customer brand experience in their attitudes and actions. Elements like brand understanding, pride of association, and referral willingness or behavior are terrific indicators of the quality of brand equity amongst the employee population.

Depending on the nature of the product or the company, you might also look at societal perspectives on the brand. Society is the place where the brand and corporate reputation intersect. Is the brand considered to be a good corporate citizen? Is it known as an active, contributing member of the community? These measures are often seen to be like placing water into buckets in advance of a fire breaking out. When something adverse happens in the marketplace — like a chemical truck overturning, a microscopic contamination of a food supply chain, or product tampering on a wide scale — the media will relentlessly whip consumers into a frenzied call for heads to roll. If you haven't stored up goodwill within the community, one minor event can spiral out of control and cost billions in lost sales and market value.

Similarly, you may need to keep water in the bucket of regulatory agencies just in case a fire breaks out in the legislature. If your long-term plan anticipates petitioning these bodies for permission to do business in new ways or raise rates at some point in the future, you'll want to ensure the field has been suitably fertilized before you plant those seeds. This can be a significant value lever for the company and a very tangible competitive advantage.

The investor perspective is also often critical. Not only is it related to the short-term cost of borrowing as we discussed above, but somewhere built into the investor's perspective is the quality of management. This is where lists like *Fortune*'s "Most Admired Companies" come in. While this is often a lagging indicator (behind customers and employees), it is nevertheless highly correlated with premium company valuation.

Companies who depend upon their broadly known corporate brand (e.g., Home Depot, Wal-Mart, or Citigroup) should constantly measure the societal corporate reputation space. It doesn't matter too much how Tootsie Roll is regarded by society at large, but if you have 300,000 employees, you are very visible in the community and will need to have public opinion on your side at one point or another.

In regulated industries, it may be government agency opinions that count. Brand equity represents a very pragmatic understanding of how much influence this company has among people that matter. And those people may matter because they're able to influence regulation or they may matter because they influence decision making in terms of investments. Arthur Andersen is a good example. This was a company that had spent all their energy generating goodwill with their customers. But when they found themselves in the midst of a public relations firestorm, they had no water in the buckets of positive brand equity among the societal and investor communities.

When you look at the strategy General Electric described in a recent article in *Fortune* magazine, Jeff Immelt, the chairman, identified three things he wants GE remembered for: innovation, efficiency, and virtue.[3] Here's a company that understands the multidimensional game in which it is engaged. When the stakes are that high, reputation becomes a kind of currency that gives you permission in a corporate sense in the same way your corporate brand gives you permission in a consumer sense. If your CEO has emphasized the importance of any or all of these additional constituencies in your company's success plan, be sure to reflect the important diagnostic and predictive elements of it on your brand scorecard.

CASE STUDY

THE ELI LILLY APPROACH
USING A BRAND SCORECARD TO ADVANCE THE CORPORATE BRAND

There's no doubt that pharmaceutical brands have become household names, especially since drug manufacturers started advertising their latest cures directly to consumers. Any TV watcher can tick off a list of popular medicinal remedies, from Allegra to Viagra, from Prevacid to Prozac. But the labs behind labels rarely come to the consumer's mind. Why? Because pharmaceutical marketers have neglected corporate branding.

Eli Lilly and Co. decided to put an internal push behind its corporate brand as products like Cialis, an erectile dysfunction medication, entered the dialect of drug therapies and other promising pharmaceuticals filled the company's R&D pipeline. Their reasoning was that a strong corporate brand lends credibility to new and competitive products, and few industries today experience the cutthroat competition that pharmaceuticals do. Pressure comes not only from other pharmaceutical developers but from the Food and Drug Administration and Medicare, as well as the managed-care organizations and health insurance providers that control its marketshare.

For four or five years, Lilly executives counted the building of a corporate reputation among their top organizational initiatives and discussed the coming brand-to-action process with employees at all levels.

Constituency Research

In 2002, Lilly conducted research about the perception of its brand from the inside out. It wanted to use employees to activate the corporate brand, so it supplemented standard customer satisfaction results with the insight of Lilly's workforce. Once it set its aims against employee reports, it launched internal training sessions led by senior managers across the business to teach employees how to act in accordance with the emerging corporate brand. It wanted their behaviors to reflect customer desires of an experience with Lilly.

Additional research conducted through this process gathered the impressions of physicians and managed-care organizations to understand how close Lilly was to delivering on its newly defined brand promise and where its commitment didn't seem evident at all.

The Eli Lilly & Co. corporate brand has four platforms on which it acts:
- *developing breakthrough products;*
- *owning medical expertise;*
- *listening and responding actively to customers; and*
- *being reliable and trustworthy in all business practices.*

The Brand-to-Action Process

Once employees completed the brand-to-action training, they went forth with new objectives that were measured by group and accessible to brand managers and the 27 top executives on a brand health scorecard. The findings were reviewed quarterly.

Employee surveys solicited information on the effectiveness of the training, asking:
- *Have you heard about Lilly's corporate branding initiative?*
- *Have you attended training on it?*
- *Has the training made an impact on the way you do your job? If so, how?*

The results exposed the brand champions and the slackers among senior management to Sherrie Bossung, manager of the corporate brand, and the corporate suite. Eighty percent of employees responded positively to the survey, confirming their exposure to the brand plan and their involvement in bringing it to the market. But that alone did not signal improvement in the organization's branding.

Employees subsequently answered questions on the value of the training to their everyday responsibilities and on their ability to make a difference in market perception of the brand.

Governance Structure and Rollout

What surprised the corporate branding team was that the more employees learned and understood the corporate brand, the more they challenged their managers and the senior executives on corporate brand strategy and implementation. Front-line employees long had seen where the Lilly brand fell short on meeting customer expectations but had little success in convincing senior management of external

---

FIGURE 6.1 — ELI LILLY'S BRAND SCORECARD

Outputs			
		(% favorable)	
	'02 Research	Dec. '03 Results	'04 Target Revised
Employee Awareness/Perceptions			
■ Recall All Four Attributes+		(XX%)	XX%
■ Recall of Breakthrough Products+		(XX%)	
■ Recall of Medical Expertise+		(XX%)	
■ Recall of Active Listening and Responding+		(XX%)	
■ Recall of Reliable and Trustworthy+		(XX%)	
■ Recall of Tagline+	(XX%)	(XX%)	XX%
■ Belief Lilly Is Living the Brand++		(XX%)	XX%
■ Perceived Value and Impact++	(XX%)	(XX%)	XX%
Employee Brand Action			
■ Seen Changes in Int'l/Ext'l Interactions++	(XX%)	(XX%)	XX%
■ Brand Event Participation		(XX%)	XX%
■ Impact of Brand Emphasis on Job		(XX%)	XX%
External Focus			
■ External Focus Metric		(XX%)	XX%

disappointments with the company. Once Lilly defined its identity and enlisted employees to build it in the marketplace, reps and researchers and all the others whose input was sloughed off previously had a greater ear into which to shout the complaints they heard.

The corporate branding initiative not only enlarged the ear of Lilly's leadership but the eye of it, too. Where the company once saw only numbers — sales revenue — it began to see the progression of the sales process. And this eye-opening led to expanded metrics, including measures of the impact of product success and the influence of the brand on customer relationships. Lilly realized that while it may

Performance

	'03 Baseline	'04 Results	'05 Target		'04 Baseline	'05 Target
Wall Street				**Phys. Brand Equity**		
■ Breakthrough	XX%	XX%	XX%	■ Overall Preference	XX	XX
■ Expertise		XX%	XX%	■ Breakthrough	XX	XX
■ Listening	XX%	XX%	XX%	■ Expertise	XX	XX
■ Trustworthy	XX%	XX%	XX%	■ Listening	XX	XX
				■ Trustworthy	XX	XX
Alliances						
■ Listening	XX%	XX%	XX%			
■ Trustworthy	XX%	XX%	XX%			
Patient Brand Equity						
■ Overall Preference		XX	XX			
■ Breakthrough		XX	XX			
■ Expertise		XX	XX			
■ Listening		XX	XX			
■ Trustworthy		XX	XX			
Payer Brand Equity						
■ Overall Preference			XX			
■ Breakthrough			XX			
■ Expertise			XX			
■ Listening			XX			
■ Trustworthy			XX			

Footnotes:
+ Employee POP scores based on a representative sample of largest 10 markets: U.S., Mexico, Germany, Spain, Italy, Canada, Japan, Australia, France, and U.K.
++ Composite score of multiple attributes

have made its numbers with some accounts in the past, it had hurt its customer equity.

Looking Inward: Eli Lilly's Scorecard

Senior management has changed its focus as a result. The company of scientists and analytical thinkers had to see data and numbers attached to brand influence before they took brand and customer equity seriously. Just a couple of years ago, Lilly didn't measure corporate brand equity at all and rationalized each weakness exposed by customer satisfaction surveys as a market fault, not a Lilly problem. The use of a dashboard has cemented dedication to the corporate brand and Lilly has launched additional workshops that attempt to change market perceptions of the company through better employee training and empowerment.

More recently, Lilly's marketing strategy folks have merged the brand health scorecard onto a dashboard that also tracks product equities. In this first marketing cycle with the tool, they look in tandem at what people think of their products as well as what they think of Lilly, mapping both to sales trends, and develop strategies that advance the performance of the entire equation rather than improving product sales at the expense of long-term customer and brand value. These strategies include customer segmentation and account-specific marketing messages that reflect the needs and wants of individual customer relationships.

This new, personalized voice motivates greater sales and encourages customers to see value in Lilly, not just its products. It has turned the process of marketing products into the practice of marketing the corporation, which can be leveraged to build product brands.

Lilly's corporate brand speaks to several constituencies, not just customers. It has acted as an internal change agent, affecting employees and increasing their confidence in and loyalty to Lilly. It has benefited Lilly's recruiting efforts, drawing potential employees to Lilly as a caring, innovative, ethical place to work. It has aided the formation of new alliances with biotech firms. And it has engaged managed-care directors who now see Lilly as a trustworthy and reputable firm.

Finding the Drivers of Success

Now that you have the framework for the many dimensions of brand equity that might be important in creating asset value, how do you tell which ones are the most predictive of financial outcomes? The most common approach is attribute correlation and covariance.

To begin, let's say you have a tracking study out in the market in which you've identified 15 key brand attributes and have a sampling of customers and prospects rating your brand vs. competitors on each attribute. You survey 100 people each month and read the results on a rolling three-month basis.

Your tracking study should include gathering self-reported information on the volume (and/or type) of purchase activity each respondent has had in the category for the past month, quarter, year — whatever timeframe is relevant to purchase cycles in your category. You are interested in understanding the purchase patterns across you and your competitors.

Now, using statistical regression techniques, you can correlate brand attribute ratings to purchase activity or purchase intentions to identify the attributes that are most strongly associated with increased category or brand purchase behavior.

Simple, right? Hardly.

There are a great many places where this approach can get derailed or become seriously misleading.

First off, self-reported purchase behavior can be significantly different from actual purchase behavior. Sometimes, people forget how much they bought and which brands. Other times they tell little white lies to protect themselves from the judgment of others (even the interviewer). If you can connect a specific individual's survey responses back to that person's actual purchase behavior as reflected in your transactional files, you can close the gap somewhat. If not, you might consider conducting a separate study specifically among a group of category consumers and check to see how self-reported behavior varies from actual purchases, then use that as an error factor to adjust what you get from your tracking studies.

Second, attributes are commonly "lumped" together by consumers into positive and negative buckets, making it difficult to see any one attribute as a real driver to a greater degree than others. This is the covariance effect — a statistical term indicating the extent to which two or more elements move in the same direction. Sometimes it's helpful to group attributes with high covariance into "factors," or higher-level descriptions. For example, the attributes "offers good value for the money" and "is priced competitively" might be grouped into a factor called "price appeal." As long as you aren't grouping so many attributes together into a few still undistinguishable factors, you can still get a strong feeling for which elements of the brand scorecard might be most important.

There are many more ways that this process can become subtly misleading. If you're not a research professional or statistician, you might consider consulting one of each in your methodology design. But, time and again, interviews with researchers suggest that the best approaches start with exhaustive qualitative research among customers and prospects to identify the possible list of driver attributes and articulate them in ways that are clear and distinct to survey respondents.

Done correctly, this effort can help focus the brand scorecard on the specific aspects of brand equity that have the greatest potential to drive incrementally profitable customer relationships. Find those nuggets, and you've got the makings of a powerful brand scorecard.

Permission: The Brand Frontier

One final candidate for a well-rounded brand scorecard is brand permission. Permission is the degree to which the target customers would be receptive to seeing the brand associated with new or related products or services. Earlier, we raised the example of Reebok and water. Reebok had no consumer permission in the water category, but they may have had a great deal of it in exercise equipment, non-apparel sporting goods, or even publishing.

If you have a desire to identify ways to extend a powerful brand into new areas, your brand scorecard should measure the degree to which the target customer is receptive to the idea. This is also captured through surveys, and subject to the same challenges as the surveys discussed above. Just because the consumer says they think your brand could add value to their perceptions of diesel engines doesn't mean they'll switch. But if it's critically important to develop permission in one or more areas of strategic interest, then it's probably worthy of including on your brand scorecard (along with volumetrics) as a leading indicator of potential developing sectors.

CONCLUSION

The brand scorecard tracks asset development that often lies between spending and profit realization. It points to the leading indicators of future profits to be realized in terms as specific as possible. This uniquely complex responsibility warrants a separate-but-linked position within the marketing dashboard where the predictive elements can be refined in the context of all the other critical learning, and not isolated as a series of "intermediary" metrics expressed in marketing mumbo jumbo.

An effective brand scorecard includes:

- customer and prospect perceptions of the most meaningful brand attributes, often including those relating to functional attributes, availability, personality, and price/value;
- perspectives of other important constituencies including employees, the community, regulators, and the investment community;
- measures of brand value to gauge the longer-term component of value created by brand investments; and
- some reflection of brand valuation monitoring for acquired brands or those likely to be sold at some point in the foreseeable future.

SOURCES

1. *MarketingNPV Journal*, vol. 2, issue 3.

2. Ambler, Tim, Senior Fellow, London Business School.

3. Gunther, Marc, *Money and Morals at GE*, *Fortune* magazine, November 15, 2004.

The Metrics You're Most Likely to Forget

The greatest insight often comes from unexpected places. We think that's true of the mixture of metrics you'll eventually select for your marketing dashboard. In Chapter 5, we covered the more conventional examples of metrics that you might install after customizing them to fit your business. In Chapter 6, we discussed the brand metrics best depicted on the brand scorecard. In this chapter, we'll examine some critical metrics you may not have considered for your marketing dashboard but that may be among the most insightful and predictive you'll install.

There are quite literally hundreds of prospective dashboard metrics to consider, but only a few that will provide any leading-indicator insight. The goal here is to point out some of the places where we normally find high correlations to company profitability. Some of these measures are often viewed as tangential to "marketing" but are, in fact, very much related to the quality and effectiveness of marketing activities. Others are frequently dismissed as "softer" measures, but are nonetheless critical to a foundation of success. Keep in mind, only you can determine which of these are right for your dashboard.

Let's begin with one of the most often overlooked areas: channel management.

Channel Metrics

If you have various distribution channels for your products, then your success is largely dependent upon the strength of those channels. The right channel metrics can monitor your progress at shaping, influencing, and managing your business to ensure the end customer is getting the best brand experience and you are getting the best return on your channel investments. Here are a few potential channel metrics to consider.

Channel Coverage

If you're selling wireless phones through independent retailers, you'll want to make sure you're covering all the places where people are buying those phones. Companies that manage their distribution chains contractually — through independent agents, sales representatives, or other partners that help them get business done — can get clarity on prospect reach and market penetration from a dashboard metric on this issue. It can be even more forward-looking if coverage incorporates prospective channel partners in various stages of finalizing agreements and building out facilities.

Channel Relationship Mix

With the level of decentralization and outsourcing in business today, companies may not have full control over the players who staff their distribution channels downstream. Major oil companies like Shell and ExxonMobil don't manage every stop on their distribution chains anymore, but they still have to keep track of how their products are selling at the consumer level. Monitoring the evolving mix of channel relationship types helps to keep the focus on the strategic importance of channel leverage strategies.

Relative Channel Performance

When you have multiple types of channels, you can often structure ways to look at marketing returns by channel — which gives you a view toward opportunities to optimize investments across channels. You might, for example, find that the cost-per-sale in one channel is significantly lower than the others. This raises the question of how much more money could be spent in selling through that channel before the returns begin to diminish (an optimization challenge). Monitoring these relative channel performance measures can provoke key questions about how resources are being allocated and help forecast the need for revitalizing efforts or planning capital investments.

Channel Stock Positions

Stock-outs can be a critically limiting factor to growth. Customers get annoyed when they go out of their way to come in only to find

FIGURE 7.1 — RELATIVE CHANNEL PERFORMANCE

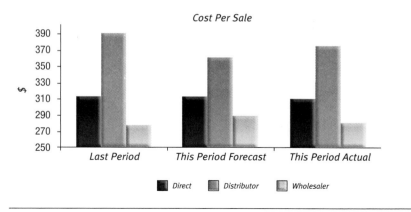

Cost Per Sale

Direct   Distributor   Wholesaler

you're out of something they think you should have. The loss can be permanent. If monitoring and forecasting in- and out-of-stock ratios is crucial to your business, then it's relevant for your dashboard. The forward-looking component of this measurement relies on good sales forecasting (see Chapter 3) to help you spot problems with your inventory before they happen. It can also help you better manage the range of merchandise you carry and watch your inventory turns more closely.

Channel Perceptions of Marketing

There's been very little dashboard activity in this area to date, but this is a measurement category worthy of careful consideration. Many of the same companies that spend millions on research to understand customer and employee views spend nothing on capturing channel perspectives. This is not only crucial to businesses like fast food franchisors and automobile manufacturers who must coordinate local marketing activity with regional co-ops of franchisees, but can be equally important to manufacturers of all types selling through Lowe's, Target, or other retailers for which the opinions of the category buyers and the sales floor associates can make or break marketing effectiveness. It's also important to industries that distribute through agent networks, wholesalers, or independent sales organizations.

Channel Power Measures

There are a number of different ways you can measure channel power, but the most compelling is how much margin you're keeping vs. your channel partners. If the markup to the final consumer is greater than the wholesale markup, it stands to reason that you have ceded some significant power to the channel. Reclaiming some of that margin is a worthy pursuit for marketing and monitoring and forecasting channel power gives you some sense of how effective you are at changing bottom-line performance through brand building or product innovation.

FIGURE 7.2 — CHANNEL POWER

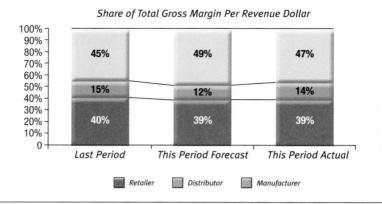

Share of Total Gross Margin Per Revenue Dollar

Organizational Metrics

In Chapter 3, we introduced you to the strategy map as a tool for aligning the role of marketing with the company and clarifying the requisite business processes, information flows, and organizational skills, tools, and culture.

It seems paradoxical, therefore, that the same companies that spend millions of dollars each year on training and development completely overlook marketing organizational effectiveness on their marketing dashboards. We don't hear too many arguments that the relationship between employees and customers is critical to the business, nor do we hear anyone bemoan the value of a better-skilled, more efficient workforce. So if it's really important to you that your organization is staffed with the right people with the right skills focused on the right things, you should be looking for dashboard elements to measure your progress.

But which organizational dashboard metrics tell you the most? The following are just a few examples.

Staffing Considerations

A dashboard can highlight whether you're working at full complement and deploying the available capital effectively. You might elect
to reflect this as a simple percentage of approved headcount filled,
or perhaps segmented on a percentage basis by newly filled vs.
trained vs. highly experienced people. Or you might choose to be
more forward-looking by monitoring hours worked by current staff
vs. approved complement as a means of forecasting overtime costs
or just highlighting potential staff burnout by correlating total hours
to historical and forecast turnover or tenure rates.

Another important dimension of staffing is skill sets. Many companies
emerge from the strategy-mapping process with great clarity on the
skills their department will need to hit its objectives. They then
engage a training company or university to develop a curriculum to
improve the specific desired skills either broadly across the marketing
organization or in narrow pockets of specific expertise. Using the
dashboard to monitor penetration of your target employees that
have achieved the requisite or desired level of training, education,
certification, or skill proficiency is mission critical and very appropriate. Skill proficiency is actually a great metric for the dashboard if
you believe that training is a forerunner for success.

Succession eligibility is another great monitoring metric for the overall
health of the organization. There are two ways to view succession
eligibility: first, as the percentage of your senior staff who have

FIGURE 7.3 — SKILL PROFICIENCY

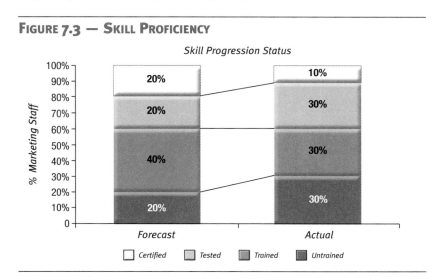

groomed replacements ready to step in for them, or second, as the overall percentage of marketing staff who are ready to step up to the next job if they had to. Either of these can be presented in stages of readiness ranging from not-at-all to ready-to-go, which will give you a more dimensional feeling for the progress your organization is making.

If success in your organization is directly related to employee proficiency and satisfaction, then monitoring employee feedback on your dashboard can be a terrific leading indicator. Many organizations have formal voice of the employee (VOE) programs that survey the employee population frequently on their knowledge, understanding, and enthusiasm for the company's mission and strategy. Others choose to measure overall job satisfaction as the likelihood of referring a friend or family member to buy from or work for the company in the next 90 days. These make strong dashboard metrics to the degree they can be correlated to marketplace success.

Innovation

As we write this book, growth is the predominant component of most CEOs' strategies. They are looking for new products, new customers, new markets, and new sources of profitable revenue. So why aren't more CMOs putting metrics for their product pipeline on a dashboard?

FIGURE 7.4 — VOICE OF THE EMPLOYEE

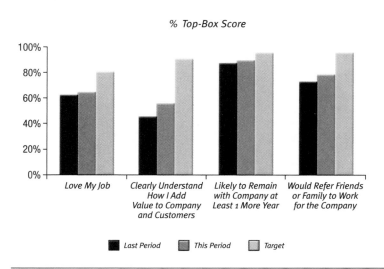

% Top-Box Score

Love My Job · Clearly Understand How I Add Value to Company and Customers · Likely to Remain with Company at Least 1 More Year · Would Refer Friends or Family to Work for the Company

■ Last Period   ■ This Period   ☐ Target

FIGURE 7.5 — INNOVATION PIPELINE

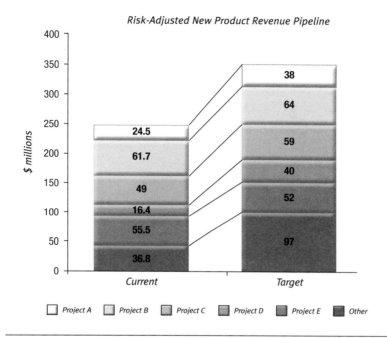

Risk-Adjusted New Product Revenue Pipeline

You can use a dashboard effectively to monitor the risk-adjusted revenue forecasts for products or services in various stages of market readiness. At a glance, this will give you terrific insight into the probability of meeting your long-term organic growth objectives. If the pipeline looks like it's stalling, you'll get an early warning indicator with sufficient time to put more resources on solving the problems or expanding the search for new opportunities.

Your dashboard is also an excellent way to track the percentage of marketing resources being spent on new product work. It helps to forecast the expected return from product development and compare it, at a glance, to the return derived from other marketing initiatives. In the end, the dashboard helps determine if innovation is being taken seriously in your organization.

Critical Project Progress

If you're building a data warehouse to transform your marketing process and strategy, you should consider monitoring that project plan on your dashboard. If you're consolidating multiple brands, sales forces, or distribution channels during a merger, then metrics that describe the stage-gates in those processes are terrific candidates to include. Whatever is important — really important — should appear on your dashboard, if you can dissect it into stages of completion, dollars, timelines, or all of the above.

Environmental Metrics

There are many variables in the business environment that can mean the difference between success and failure. Obviously, the environmental variables affecting your business will be different from those in another industry or category. Here are a few of the more common considerations worthy of dashboard inclusion.

Market Growth

The health of your current markets is a critical barometer of future performance. How fast is your category growing? How many net new customers are coming into the category each day/week/month? Is the consumption pattern per customer changing for the better? Are they changing for the worse? Category health metrics like these should give you a clear sense of any rising or falling tides that may lift or crash your boat.

FIGURE 7.6 — CATEGORY HEALTH

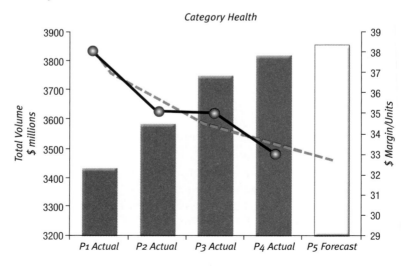

Competitive Health

Start tracking the margins of your competitors with every source of information you have. A dashboard is perfect for a constant reading on the ratio between how fast your products are growing and how fast your category is growing overall. It may be nice to know that the sales of a particular product of yours were growing by 8% a year, but a shock to find out that the category was growing by 12% and you were losing share all along.

You also need to find a way to track pricing at retail (or the final sale to end users) across you and your competitors. Keeping an eye on category price elasticity can be a strong leading indicator of purchase trends and keep you in a proactive stance on margin management. While you're at it, consider burrowing into the overall category pricing structure. This goes further than comparisons at retail to monitor how wholesale prices are moving and how raw material pricing projections might create a threat to your product pipeline and ultimately affect future costs.

Also keep an eye out for potential mergers among competitors that may decimate your channel power or shut you out of key customers.

Monitor your substitute categories of products closely to help forecast market tightening. In the chemical business, for example, there's often more than one compound that a manufacturer can use to reach a certain end result. Knowing how prices are moving in each compound class can keep you ahead of the demand curve for your own products.

You might also monitor the entry/exit barriers to your business. If the cost to enter your business starts to fall, be prepared for more competition. If it rises, better times could be ahead.

Weather

This should be self-explanatory. If weather has a big impact on your business, track weather forecasts closely. Not that we're suggesting weather is a good dashboard metric, but the long-range temperature and precipitation indices are often important elements of sales forecasts and even more often very insightful diagnostic tools.

FIGURE 7.7 — SUBSTITUTION PRICE ELASTICITIES

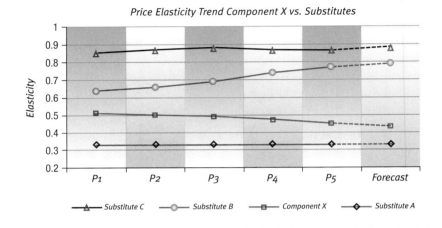

Price Elasticity Trend Component X vs. Substitutes

There are dozens of companies specializing in providing detailed weather forecast data. Find the one that offers it in a form most applicable to your needs.

Trends and Demographics

Looking at the evolution of the world around you is critical. You might want to know the demographic data on who's been buying your product and whether that information is likely to undergo significant change. Changes in fashion, hairstyles, automobile engineering, family dynamics, music, and many other facets of life can have definitive impacts on businesses selling raw materials or component parts far upstream from the end consumable.

Tracing your product or service from your point of delivery through to its very end user can be extremely helpful in identifying the potentially disruptive forces at work around you and focusing attention on how to monitor them most effectively.

Macroeconomics

Consumer confidence and energy price forecasts are important to most companies, but depending on your business, public health projections, savings rates, or interest-rate forecasts might have more relevant meaning.

Macroeconomics is one of the easiest areas to find statistical correlations to your sales or profits. Most macroeconomic factors are tracked in time series by some governmental or educational institution and the data is cheap, if not free. If you haven't done so yet, you might want to hire an academic consultant to test for some correlations for your company as a means of challenging conventional wisdom and identifying the emerging changes in your business in the larger economic context.

Start by developing a long list of hypotheses about which macroeconomic factors *might* be drivers of your business. Then review the list with your university consultants to see what they might add and ask them to run some correlations. Based on what they come back with, look to refine your hypotheses further, and, after a few iterations, you'll likely hone in on the best environmental leading indicators.

Geopolitics

In a world gripped by 24-hour news and volatile events at home and abroad, it never hurts to keep an eye on how economic and social events affect the spending of money. The effect September 11th had on the investment and travel industries worldwide still lingers in the minds of many marketers, not to mention their customers. The dashboard is not an ideal place to track geopolitical events, but it can be a great way to monitor long-term shifts in political ideologies as a pre-cursor to anticipated changes in governments, consumer attitudes and behaviors, or regulatory changes. One company we know closely monitors an index of consumer "values," which it has found to be correlated to future sales of its publications. There are plenty of syndicated research services out there tracking many dimensions of these variables. If you can't find one already existing that meets your needs, consider investing in a custom approach or launching a collaborative industry effort.

Media

The advent of major media-tracking databases has made it much easier to track ideas and opinions in the world today. If your business is heavily influenced by how people think or feel about a particular issue, you can quickly establish a tracking approach to measure the number of times the issue is mentioned in the media by day, by media channel, by geographic territory, etc.

FIGURE 7.8 — SAMPLE ENVIRONMENTAL LEADING INDICATORS

Competitive Activity
- ❏ *Spending or share-of-voice*
- ❏ *Shipments*
- ❏ *Sales recruiting*
- ❏ *Facility construction permits*

Weather

Macroeconomic
- ❏ *Interest rates*
- ❏ *Housing starts*
- ❏ *Unemployment claims*
- ❏ *Consumer price index*
- ❏ *Consumer confidence index*

Demographics
- ❏ *Popular aging*
- ❏ *Disposable income*

Geopolitical
- ❏ *U.S. State Department warnings*
- ❏ *Trade account balances*

Societal
- ❏ *Marital trends/divorce rates*
- ❏ *Commuting time*

Cultural
- ❏ *Music downloads*
- ❏ *Dining out frequency*

Media
- ❏ *Article mentions*
- ❏ *Story frequency*

Regulatory
- ❏ *Legislation status*
- ❏ *Election trends*

Alternatively, you can use the same services to track your own brand or industry and monitor the number of positive or negative mentions you are getting. This is especially helpful if you are intent on measuring the effectiveness of a public affairs or media relations program.

Regulation

Most businesses operate under government regulations. In fact, most operate under *many* government regulations. The majority of them aren't a direct concern for the marketing dashboard, but some are. For example, compliance with consumer privacy laws is a critical marketing regulatory concern. Industry pricing collaboration can also be a crucial regulatory issue.

Tracking the regulatory environment on the marketing dashboard serves two purposes. First, it keeps the organization focused on the importance of remaining in full compliance and presents the current (and forecast) levels of compliance. Second, it serves as an important support point should you ever need to demonstrate to regulators, judiciary, or the public at large just how much emphasis you put on being a good corporate citizen.

CONCLUSION

There are hundreds of potentially insightful marketing metrics worthy of being included on your marketing dashboard, but only a few that will give you the real insight into marketing effectiveness you're looking for. We've provided a few possible starting places to look for the areas of insight where you might not have thought to look before.

Building an effective marketing dashboard is as much an exercise in creativity and problem solving as most other marketing functions. Ultimately, the quality of your dashboard is a function of your ability to identify the hidden metrics that distinguish between success and failure. Only you will know what those are. Thinking through the list presented here should help stimulate other areas of thought.

But remember ... the effectiveness of your dashboard is likely to be inversely proportional to the number of metrics you put on it. Your objective is to find the fewest number of metrics to tell the story that needs telling.

CHAPTER 8

How to Overcome Data Deficiency: Sound Approaches to Fill the Void

There is a measurement frenzy going on in marketing today. This is admirable, even altruistic. To meet the goals of top management, marketers are digging up more data than ever, applying rocket-science analytics to it, and believing that the resulting numbers will speak for themselves.

But what's really going on, even in organizations with enough sophistication and money to make great things happen, is the biggest mistake in marketing measurement today. Companies are focused on what they *can* measure instead of what they *should* measure.

Throughout this book, we've been talking about weaning yourself from past-performance data as your primary measurement system. In this chapter, we're going to share some important tools and techniques to accomplish that.

Does This Sound Like Your Organization?

CMO: "I'm getting some pressure to report on the return we're getting from our marketing spending."

VP: "We don't have that data, but what we do have are advertising spending by media, brand awareness tracking studies, and sales by division for each of the past six quarters."

CMO: "Well, won't that give us a good view into the question?"

VP: "We could build a media-mix model to see which campaigns are generating the best results and then adjust our plans to duplicate the successes."

CMO: "OK, go do that."

Six Months Later...

VP: "The media-mix model says that for every dollar we invest in advertising, we're getting $14.23 in incremental sales."

CMO: "That's huge! Now we can go to finance and tell them that if they give us that extra $10 million in ad budget, we'll bring home *$140 million* in sales!"

VP: "Well … not exactly. We did look at message saturation levels, and we still have some room to improve before hitting those. But what we didn't look at was what an *extra* $10 million might do since it would have to include an assessment of not just how we'd spend it, but how the competitors might respond and how our channel partners would adjust their plans. It's a tricky problem, but we could solve it with another six months and some more modeling."

CMO: "Will that answer the original question about what we're getting from our marketing spending?"

VP: "Sort of. There will always be some wiggling in the assumptions underlying the model. And I'm already sensing that finance isn't buying into the whole approach."

CMO: "Well, then, we'd better push harder to fill the gaps."

"Filling in the gaps" — remember that phrase. It's exactly the right thing to do. Somehow, you need to reach beyond the data at your fingertips to find answers to the really hard questions like, "What return am I getting on marketing spending?" But be particularly careful, as the same rationale often leads to the following potential dangers:

1. **Establishing artificial metrics:** This happens when the search for mathematical answers to tough problems feeds the marketer's innate desire for simple solutions. Absent some sort of magic formula that fully predicts bottom-line impact from marketing spending, there is a strong tendency to stop short and settle for predicting such intermediary metrics as awareness, preference, persuasion, repurchase intentions, and other key stops on the path to profitability. Not only does this effort fail

to address the original question of marketing's impact on the bottom line, it leaves the rest of the company unfulfilled in its desire to really understand the link between marketing and profitability. Worse, it reinforces the jargon of marketing and builds higher, thicker walls between the people who really understand these concepts and those who don't.

2. **Framing too narrowly:** What's the problem with focusing only on areas for which data is readily available? First, you will at best be reinforcing the current ways of looking at and managing the business. If your framework is restricted to what you have data for, you are perpetuating the limitations of the business, not expanding its reach. Second, you risk creating an illusion of progress. People want to go home at night feeling like they've accomplished something each day. That puts a significant amount of emotional pressure on you to use the tools and information at your fingertips. But if you cave in to this desire to "just get something done," you wind up allocating all your precious resources and fail to break the cycle of familiarity. Besides, once you've picked all the low-hanging analytical fruit, top management will still be hungry for answers to questions you haven't yet attempted to answer.

3. **Being precisely wrong:** Science can be dangerous. Analytical tools, even in the hands of those who are well-trained in their application, are still wholly dependent upon the quality of the hypotheses against which they're applied. Start with a vague hypothesis and you will likely end up with a very specific answer that may cause you to solve the wrong problem. Time, money, and credibility are squandered in the process.

Understand Why You Don't Have the Data

Before you try the approaches we suggest in this chapter, it makes sense to try to understand the reasons *why* the data you think you need to measure marketing isn't available. Asking this question may force some essential critical thinking about what you're really trying to accomplish and the staffing and resource issues at the root of the problem.

The fishbone exercise is an analysis tool that provides a systematic way of looking at problems and the contributing factors. It's also called a "cause-and-effect diagram."

Here's how it works:

FIGURE 8.1 — FISHBONE DIAGRAM

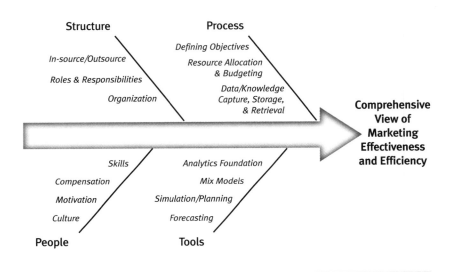

---

1. Decide on the main problem or issue you want to study — and put it at the head of the fish. You might define that problem as "Inability to Measure Marketing Effectiveness" and use the rest of the skeleton to highlight obstacles to be overcome. You can also take a more positive spin by using a label like "Achieving Full Accountability for Marketing Investments" at the head and using the rest of the diagram to identify all the required steps and sub-components of success.

2. As you can see, each bone of the fish has a category label. Major categories might include people, process, tools, resources, systems, or suppliers. Use whatever headings relate to what you've written at the head of the fish.

3. Start brainstorming with your team to identify the factors within each major category that may be affecting the problem.

The question to ask is: "What are the issues affecting this category?" Be particularly careful to not let the dominant personalities in the group steer the exercise in parochial directions.

4. Work backward up each fishbone to write down sub-factors. Keep asking, "Why is this happening?" until you no longer get useful information.

5. Analyze the results of the fishbone after team members agree that the chart is complete. Do this by looking for those items that appear in more than one major category. These repeaters become your most likely causes. These discoveries should create the foundation for an action plan for how to proceed without data.

Another good thing about the fishbone exercise is that it's a great way to bring in constituents from outside the marketing department — finance, sales, or SBU leaders — to get them to talk about their own departmental measurement challenges. You listen to their problems, they listen to yours, and soon you have allies in your process to overcome obstacles to measurement. Most importantly, they may have already come up with some novel metrics you can adapt for your specific purposes.

If there's nothing else you learn from this chapter, remember that to measure marketing effectiveness, you will have to get comfortable working without data. Treat it as the norm, not the exception. Great managers are those who get exceptional results from ordinary resources in tough circumstances. You can too if you:

■ start by developing and framing the right questions to ask;

■ plan your approach to answering them *as best you can* today, putting your best estimates on the dashboard for all to see and enhance;

■ articulate a path to continuous improvement in measurement process over time; and

■ involve the key influencers in architecting the process to ensure collaboration and acceptance.

FINDING DRIVERS WITHOUT DATA

Many times when a problem surfaces, it doesn't arrive with enough data to determine exactly what is causing it. The data vacuum is a breeding ground for opinions and theories about how to fix the problem.

Imagine a marketing promotion for a wireless telecom company that is failing due to inconsistent implementation among internal and third-party sales channels. A team of people representing the areas of marketing planning, sales, channel support, and finance have boiled down dozens of possible reasons for the failure into the following possible root causes:

A. Program not clearly defined
B. Program not integrated with other elements of the marketing plan
C. Rapid introduction has stretched resources
D. Lack of channel support capacity
E. Lack of time and resources
F. External factors driving inconsistency of execution
G. Planning approach non-standardized
H. Poor communication between business units

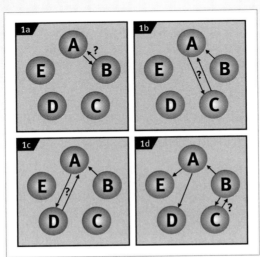

FIGURE 8.2

Sound Familiar?

A simple way the team can test the relative strength of each possible cause is to assess the relationship between each pair of variables in turn to determine whether there is a causal or influence relationship between them and in which direction the relationship might be stronger.

For example, if it compared A to B, the team might surmise that B would tend to cause A because lack of integration with other plan components would make it difficult for people to know how it fit in with the current activities and therefore make the program more confusing. If team members next compared A to C, they might find no particular causal relationship. The team would then compare A to D, A to E, and so on, drawing arrows to indicate causal relationships (see figure 8.2). After finishing with A, the team would do the comparisons with B until it had completed the entire network of relationships between the variables.

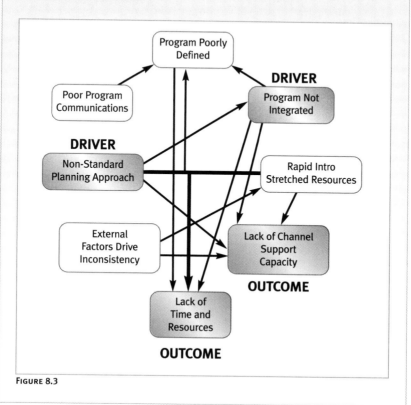

FIGURE 8.3

The final graphic (figure 8.3) would then show how many arrows were coming out of and going into each variable's box. The relationship between arrows out and arrows in is a good indicator of which variables are the drivers (most arrows out) and which are the outcomes (most arrows in). The highest priority is then placed on addressing the drivers, knowing that outcomes would improve simultaneously.

This approach, sometimes called an interrelationship diagram, can be a powerful way to get different perspectives aligned behind a common approach when facts and data are in short supply.[1]

Mining the Shadow of the Doubt

When you have the data, use it. If you're lucky enough to have the right data in the right quantities, let your analytical scientists drive and put your instincts in the passenger seat long enough to watch and learn. When you don't have the data and you can't buy it or develop a clear proxy for it from some other source, you need to know you can *make* the data yourself.

That probably sounds heretical to many of you who've invested a great deal of money and energy in beefing up your analytical capabilities. But where the analytics leave off, we succeed or fail by the quality of our guesses.

The secret lies in *response modeling*, a tool that will help you make better guesses by talking to people with the right experience.

Aside from a few purely direct-response businesses like catalog retailing, there is no business today capable of completely and comprehensively measuring marketing effectiveness without some doubt. Even the soundest efforts require that significant assumptions be made to fill the gaps in the data or deal with the uncertainties of dynamic markets.

- How will competitors react if we do X?
- Will distributors increase or decrease support?
- What are commodity prices likely to do?

Response modeling is a process that will help you forecast based on the best human expertise you have. In its simplest terms, you gather a group of people in your organization that you believe have the experience to make good guesses on specific issues you want to track. Next, you walk that group through a structured question-and-answer process — essentially a response card — in which you ask each of them very specific questions that zero in on a target with scores attached to each questions.

You might ask a group to predict where a certain product is going to be 12 months from now, then ask them to break that prediction down on a month-by-month basis. Then you ask a series of questions designed to understand the drivers of the outcome and the relationships between the variables. For example:

- What would happen to sales if we doubled our advertising?
- What would happen if we cut it in half?
- What if we see one or two competitors flood our space with similar products?
- Based on that situation, what would we see if we doubled our advertising spend? Cut it in half?

During a series of meetings over several days, the group thrashes out the most likely scenarios and debates the answers to these structured questions and the assumptions underlying them. The responses are entered into a computer model.

Example: If every manager were asked about the likely effect on profits if advertising were increased by 25%, it would produce a spectrum of possible outcomes from "no effect" (or maybe even "modest decrease") to "modest increase" to "significant increase." Those outcomes could be plotted on a curve to show the range of expected outcomes.

Now if we asked for expectations for a 25% decrease, we could also plot those. And if we continued both up and down to 50%, 75%, and 100% increases, as well as 50%, 75%, and 100% decreases, we'd have a pretty clear set of predictions that we could statistically translate into a response model.

If we wanted to get more complex, we could ask the same group to predict the outcome of simultaneously changing advertising spend *and* changing direct mail. Human beings with experience in the business will use their knowledge and intuition to develop individual best-guess outcomes. The matrix might look like this:

FIGURE 8.4 — RESPONSE GRID: CHANGE IN FORECAST SALES RELATING TO CHANGES IN ADVERTISING AND DM SPENDING

Change in ad spend/ change in DM spend	-100%	-75%	-50%	-25%	No Change	+25%	+50%	+75%	+100%
-100%	-80%	-70%	-60%	-40%	-30%	-20%	-15%	-10%	-10%
-75%	-70%	-60%	-50%	-30%	-25%	-15%	-10%	-5%	5%
-50%	-60%	-50%	-40%	-30%	-20%	-10%	-15%	5%	15%
-25%	-50%	-40%	-30%	-25%	-10%	-5%	-20%	10%	25%
No change	-40%	-30%	-20%	-20%	0%	20%	30%	50%	60%
25%	-30%	-20%	-10%	-5%	10%	10%	40%	40%	70%
50%	-20%	-10%	0%	5%	0%	40%	60%	70%	75%
75%	-10%	-10%	10%	10%	-5%	50%	60%	70%	75%
100%	-10%	0%	15%	20%	-15%	60%	70%	80%	80%

In other words, the collective perspectives of the brightest minds in the company, especially those that disagree on likely outcomes, create a universe of possible outcomes that can be represented by a mathematical algorithm that says for every change of x%+/- in ad spend, profits will change +/-y%.

The model you create represents the collective tribal wisdom on a particular issue that might otherwise be tough to turn into a metric because *you don't have the data*. In direct marketing, response models are used to forecast the likely marketplace response given a certain combination of creative messages. By varying the questions, you can come up with a response model that represents the expected success rates of various changes in inputs on desired outputs.

Response models are really nothing more than a highly structured way of helping a management team direct its experience into an aggregated best guess. This may seem unpredictable, but in reality it helps identify the subtle relationships between actions and outcomes while removing some of the risk of any single individual being wildly wrong.

Every manager can form an opinion on the likely result of a certain action or inaction solely on the basis of their experience. The cumulative experience base within a company is often the most powerful untapped data source. Harnessing those individual perspectives into a collective view often provides tremendous insight helpful in making hard decisions. Of course, this approach is vulnerable to bad guessing by the entire group (which would be the Achilles heel of the company anyway), or even to sabotage by those who have an axe to grind against a certain form of spending. But if your group is diverse enough, it's not hard to minimize these risks and improve the quality of the outcome.

The Benefit of Adding More Variables

Response models can be as simple or as complex as you'd like them to be, thanks to software now out on the market. You can also use this process to track several variables, such as brand awareness, distribution, perceived quality, or service satisfaction and see how each element has affected sales. Over time, you could measure executives' perspectives on how a single change in one variable or all of them might affect sales overall.

Today's desktop software lets us go even further — three, five, even 10 or more variables, although the process gets too arduous for the managers at some point. And the resulting response models provide the basis for forecasting what results are likely to be given proposed changes to spending patterns. In the end, this process should also yield a concise list of leading indicators that really do belong on your dashboard.

Even before you migrate your discoveries to the dashboard, another benefit from response modeling is that it can be used to build a crude version of a media-mix model for organizations without the transactional data to do so. The collective experience of the group might help define an optimal spending pattern that serves multiple constituencies.

FIGURE 8.5 — RESPONSE MODEL PROCESS

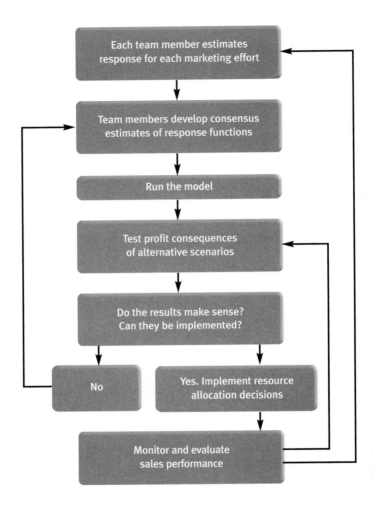

SUPERCHARGING YOUR RESULTS

You've built your response models and your collective result shows that changes in three variables — perceived product quality, price competitiveness, and service satisfaction — are most likely to drive incremental sales. With this data from the manager panel, you can build a simulation model to test the relative sensitivity of each variable as a driver of increased profits.

Desktop simulation tools like Crystal Ball® or @RISK are inexpensive (under $2000), powerful, able to plug right into Excel, and relatively easy to use if you know a normal distribution from a logarithmic one. There are even lower-priced versions like XLSim® for those who don't know the difference, but you'll trade off some flexibility.

Using one of these packages, you can fit the shape of the response curve that you received during the manager panel to one of dozens of standard probability distribution curves. You can set the upper, lower, and most-likely ranges of response, then run thousands of simulations to see which of the input variables are the biggest drivers of profits and test the degree to which they affect each other. All done right there on your desktop.

FIGURE 8.6 — MONTE CARLO SIMULATION OUTPUT

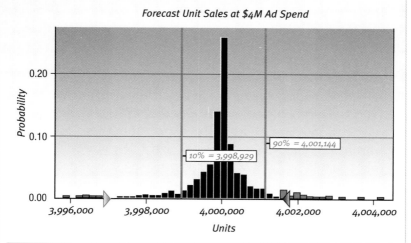

Forecast Unit Sales at $4M Ad Spend

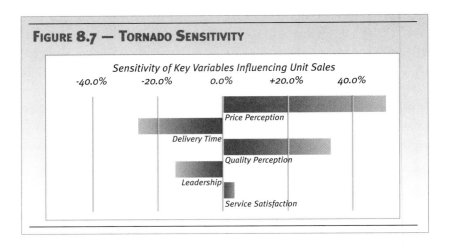

FIGURE 8.7 — TORNADO SENSITIVITY

Sensitivity of Key Variables Influencing Unit Sales

Road-Testing with Consumers

Of course, once we understand which of the variables are the drivers of profitability and how they might relate to one another, we should begin to augment our manager-panel perspective with some voice-of-the-customer research. Testing our hypothesis on real customers and even rejecters can help you validate and refine your no-data perspective, perhaps even identifying variables you missed completely.

Once validated, quantitative research can then be used to begin tracking the evolution of the key perceptual drivers on a quarterly, monthly, or even weekly basis. This data can then be compared to actual sales and marketing investment data to evolve toward a highly disciplined way of confirming predictive metrics and using them to forecast business results.

Other Ways to Forecast

We keep repeating how necessary it is that you look forward in the way you select, collect, and analyze data that will end up as metrics for your marketing dashboard. We obviously don't need analytics to measure last month's sales. They are what they are. The real questions should be, "Where did they come in vs. expectations? How do they stack up to the forecast we've created through various forms of analysis?"

Keeping the focus on performance vs. forecast serves to underscore the question of how well we have forecast our results. If our forecasts are bad, why? How can we improve them? These are the questions that stimulate organizational learning and growth. They also keep us from spending precious time determining why this period was lower than last. Who cares? We should concern ourselves with this period vs. expectations for this period and as an input into future periods.

Response modeling is the first stop on the list of techniques for doing so. There are a few others:

The Delphi Method

This method utilizes several expert panels (functional or cross-functional; preferably a mix of insiders and outsiders) who are asked to provide a forecast.[2] Each forecast is weighted equally and the results are shared between panels. The members continue the discussion in an effort to fine-tune their forecast with points raised by other panels. If the panels' forecasts begin to converge, a final forecast can be drawn from the average of all the forecasts. Otherwise, the dialogue focuses on why the divergence persists and what the key variables of divergence are.

The Delphi method is similar to building response models, but looks only at the question of convergence for reliability, not development of a predictive model.

Nielsen's BASES Model

If you have a new product to be distributed in supermarkets, drug stores, or discount stores, ACNielsen's BASES database of 25 years of product launch history might be a great starting point. The methodology looks at thousands of products with similar characteristics, consumer receptivity, and marketing plans and forecasts sales under flexible sets of assumptions. Unfortunately, BASES is limited to just these kinds of retail locations. It doesn't extend to hardware, electronics, or stores other than those in the three above categories.

The Diffusion Model

This widely used mathematical model uses rates of product adoption and usage spread from other established products to predict the rate of new product acceptance into the market. Often called the Bass diffusion model, after the professor who popularized the method, it looks at the pace of adoption of a product or service over time and maps it out as a linear function. Products with similar characteristics (categories, user segments, price points, etc.) can be used as proxies for new products by using the published coefficients of adoption and diffusion and then adjusting to fit your expectations. It is very applicable to both durable and non-durable goods across a wide variety of categories.

And there are many other approaches as well …

Figure 8.8 can help you in determining what kind of forecasting process or methodology is most likely the right one for you. Created by Professor J. Scott Armstrong of The Wharton School, it allows you to trace your way down the selection tree to find the path that best describes your situation. At the bottom, you'll see the type of forecasting process that meets your needs.

There are so many good techniques available today to help overcome data challenges. Thanks to Six Sigma and Lean, many companies are already employing these techniques, although perhaps not yet in marketing measurement. These approaches can be combined and supplemented with market research to develop a custom process that best suits your needs. Be careful to check your preferred approach with someone experienced in forecasting before you go too far down the road of time, money, or reputation to ensure your efforts are sound.

FIGURE 8.8 — SELECTION TREE FOR FORECASTING METHODS

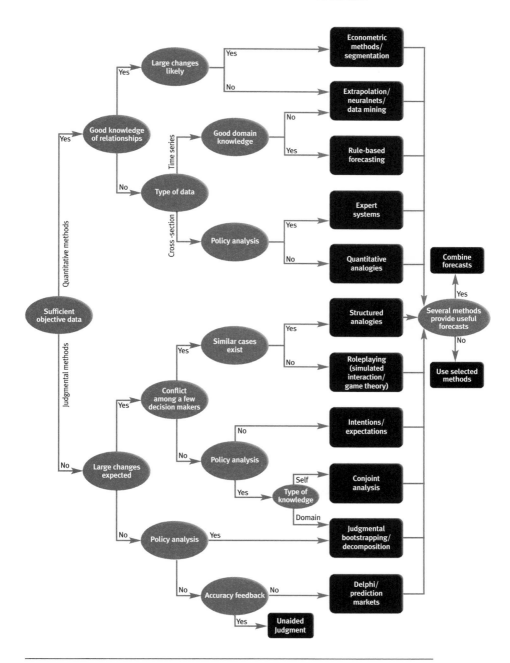

Source: Prof. J. Scott Armstrong, The Wharton School of the University of Pennsylvania, April 2005. Reprinted with permission.[3]

CONCLUSION

Not having the right data is no longer a valid excuse for leaving key business drivers off your dashboard. Find a disciplined way to get at best estimates of the data you seek. Create a continuous improvement path to begin collecting and validating it. And look to the intersection of quantitative research and basic statistical tools to help refine and enhance both your diagnostic and predictive capabilities.

While many may be concerned with the validity and reliability of these methods, the alternative of doing nothing should be of greater concern. If our approach to filling data gaps involves key stakeholders from finance, sales, and operations, the resulting models are much more likely to be both accurate and accepted as the "best we can do."

Remember that credibility is a function of accountability and perceived objectivity. Letting your executive committee know you're implementing the methods suggested in this chapter will go much further towards establishing that credibility than a dozen analysts working in secret to crack the elusive code of marketing effectiveness.

SOURCES

1. *MarketingNPV Journal*, vol. 1, issue 4.

2. *MarketingNPV Journal*, vol. 1, issue 3.

3. Armstrong, J. Scott, "The Selection Tree Forecasting Principles," 2005.

Crystal Ball is a registered trademark of Decisioneering, Inc.

XLSim is a registered trademark of AnalyCorp, Inc.

PART III

Going Live: Implementing Your Dashboard

Keep It Simple: Design the User Experience Before Committing to Execution

G ive yourself some credit: Human beings have an incredible ability to take in visual information. If the Internet has taught us anything, it's that any kind of data presented simply and sensibly speeds up our ability to read, to collect, to synthesize, and to analyze.

So, let's ask the question again — what does a dashboard do? It allows us to read, collect, synthesize, and analyze in a matter of seconds. Sometimes, it happens in a fraction of seconds. The faster, the better.

This is why the *presentation* of the metrics you choose for your marketing dashboard is just as important as the process you've taken to find them. Today, graphics are everything. Graphics — designed images — are critical to the success of the marketing dashboard because images can be absorbed into the brain quicker than the written or spoken word. After a long day of reading reports and sitting in meetings, tabular data is a turnoff. Rich, colorful charts edited to emphasize the most critical information are friendlier to the eye and more easily recorded by the brain.

This chapter will discuss how we best receive information and how to apply such concepts to the design of your dashboard. Even if your dashboard appears on a weekly sheet of paper dropped into your colleagues' inbox, the principles you'll learn here will help you make sure that sheet of paper is a must-read for everyone in your organization.

What Are You Looking at?

Your age is a telltale sign for the way you were trained to receive information. Consider that today's 60-year-old manager spent most of his formative years looking at black-and-white TV, while 23-year-olds began staring into a computer screen from the time they toddled off to preschool. The rest of us fall somewhere in the middle.

What's the point of this generational exercise? That visual acceptance of information has accelerated in the last half century to the point where visual presentation of information is a constant. We think, learn, and communicate differently because of it. That's why graphics have moved to the forefront of everything we do.

Yet as you take on the responsibility of building the marketing dashboard, understand that you can't just hand a bunch of metrics off to a graphic designer and expect her to spit back a dashboard metric that's both pretty and informative. You need to take responsibility for knowing something about the design process. You need to let that knowledge guide your selection of elements for your dashboard. This is something of a challenge because most senior managers have never had to think about the essential principles of good design for charts and graphs.

Harvard cognitive psychologist Stephen M. Kosslyn states there are three principles of the limits of visual information:[1]

1. The Mind Is Not a Camera. We may think we're recording every image in front of us, but our brains are actually very selective:

- We are attracted to brighter colors and symmetrical shapes.
- We associate elements of similar color and shape as actually being related.
- We process visual data in channels of orientation, color, and motion — changes in any one of those channels forces us to readjust the others.
- It is more difficult for us to judge things like area, intensity, and volume.
- Spatial relationships between items require more effort.
- We tend to try to interpret two-dimensional patterns as three-dimensional if possible, but not very accurately.

2. The Mind Judges a Book by Its Cover. You may be the most skeptical person on earth, but visually, you're as gullible as the day you were born:

- We trust our vision so much that we have a tendency to believe that what we see is true.

- Our basic instincts make us sensitive to changes in our visual field and we try to interpret them — which is why any perceived change in a familiar pattern is assumed to be informative.

3. The Spirit Is Willing, but the Mind Is Weak. We are only aware of our inability to detect and absorb visual information at a sub-cognitive level:

- Short-term memory is limited in how much information it can hold before we begin to get confused and make misjudgments. It's like the short-term memory is in a transitory state, much like the RAM in your computer.

FIGURE 9.1 — CAN YOU ABSORB THE MEANING OF THIS CHART?

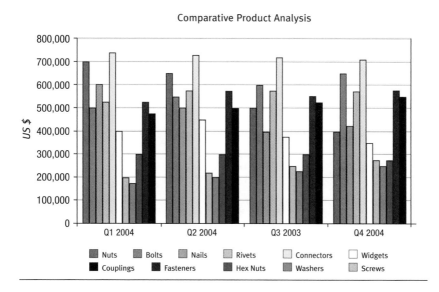

- We attempt to process new information against our stored patterns in our long-term memory, which is far from neatly cataloged. Long-term memory can surface randomly — like when you recognize your sixth-grade English teacher in the supermarket after 30 years.

- We reflexively gather information in a way to minimize the effort required to understand it. Whether we are conscious of it or not, we work to fit things into existing patterns.

- We often stop short of finding the best answer to problems we solve. It's what Nobel Prize winner Herb Simon referred to as "satisficing" — essentially accepting what you see as real. You don't choose to work any harder; you just want to accept what you see and move on.

Design Concepts for Non-Designers

Dashboard designs get into trouble most often because they overuse our short-term memory. Either due to their complexity or simple matters of bad design, a dashboard that fails to understand the psychology of our visual responses can either underwhelm or over-whelm a viewer. Your staff may look at your hard-researched metrics and move on because they don't make any kind of connection. For all the effort you're pouring into your dashboard effort, you can't afford to let this happen.

Lynd Bacon, Ph.D., President of LBA Associates, offers the term "cognitive load" to describe the energy necessary to interpret what is being visually conveyed.[2] He suggests the following ideas to guide the creation of all marketing messages:

- Don't eliminate necessary complexity. Instead, make it easy for the viewer to understand the relevancy of the complexity.

- Make the underlying technology completely transparent.

- Don't separate the viewer from the information by obfuscating it with bad design.

This is a tall order. Executives know what's in their heads and they know how to give orders. But they can't create a graphically savvy dashboard with those skills.

A case in point most of us are already familiar with — the overly busy PowerPoint presentation. Many of us already think we will be better judged if we jam as much information into each page view we present, just in case we get asked a question. Our solution? Point to the slide. The solution *should* be to draw more attention to the most important details of the communication and a dedication to communicating them simply, clearly, quickly — and attractively.

Bacon adds that the *effectiveness* of any graphical presentation equals the ability to:

- **Be understood** — Based on the presentation, the viewer can explain it with accuracy.

- **Be quick** — The viewer can absorb the information quickly, with minimal cognitive load.

- **Be remembered** — The viewer can recall the information accurately.

- **Be easy to use** — In the case of a dashboard, each level of information has to be easy to reach and easy to find.

- **Be appealing** — Like anything you want people to gravitate to, it has to look good.

- **Be illuminating** — A good presentation causes us to see what we never expected to see.

Principles in Practice

The primary purpose of the dashboard is to be able to allow you, at a glance, to see how well you're performing against other key metrics so you can quickly determine what's working and what's not. It should also allow you to see where you're going to be next month or next quarter in your performance based on current data.

Picking up on Kosslyn's ideas, we offer the following design guidelines to apply when creating a dashboard:

- Changes in size or brightness attract attention (figure 9.2).

FIGURE 9.2 — CHANGES IN SIZE OR BRIGHTNESS ATTRACT ATTENTION

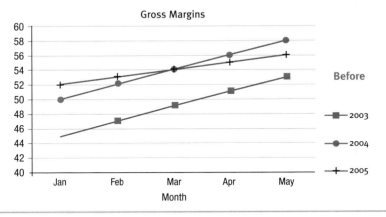

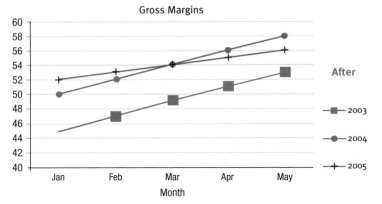

■ Elements similar in color or shape tend to get grouped into patterns and are interpreted as being similar or related (figure 9.3).

FIGURE 9.3 — USING SHAPES AND COLORS TO ASSOCIATE ELEMENTS

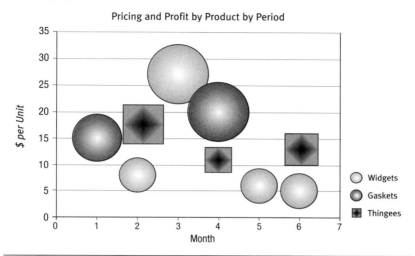

■ Warm hues suggest foreground; cooler ones, background (figure 9.4).

FIGURE 9.4 — FOREGROUND VS. BACKGROUND

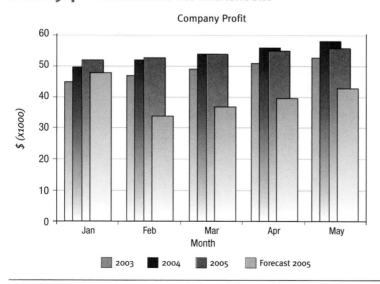

■ Keep values out of plot area if you can (figure 9.5).

FIGURE 9.5 — MOVING VALUES OUT OF PLOT AREAS

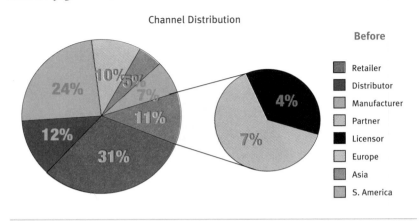

Channel Distribution

Before

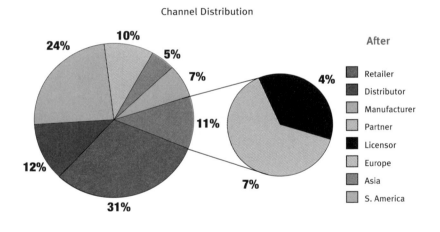

Channel Distribution

After

- Don't allow elements in any single chart to be too distant from one another — makes it harder to relate them — increasing the tendency to "dismiss" them as irrelevant (figure 9.6).

FIGURE 9.6 — CONTROLLING THE SEPARATION OF ELEMENTS

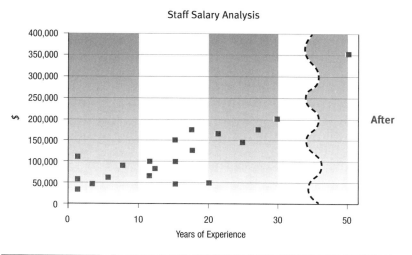

■ Design to allow maximum detection of data points. Avoid the "blob" — improve understanding of relevance between data elements (figure 9.7).

FIGURE 9.7 — AVOIDING THE "BLOB"

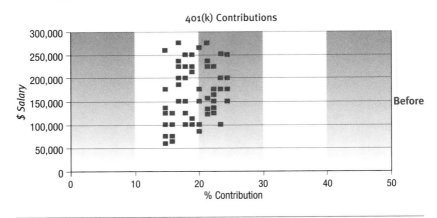

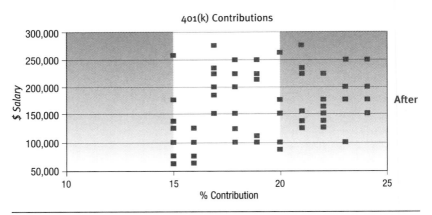

■ Watch the data/ink ratio: There needs to be a balance of information and design. An over-designed page will look too technical and an overly simplified one looks almost childish. You need the design to be inviting, but not at the expense of communicating the key information (figure 9.8).

FIGURE 9.8 — MANAGE THE DATA/INK RATIO

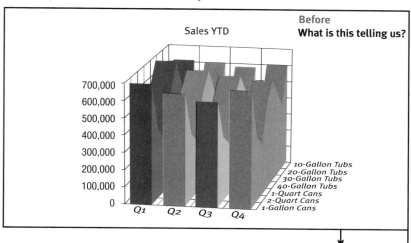

Sales YTD

Before
What is this telling us?

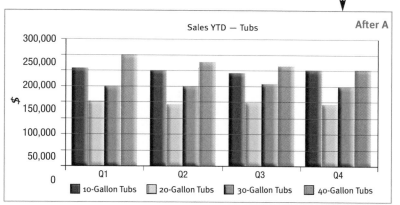

Sales YTD — Tubs

After A

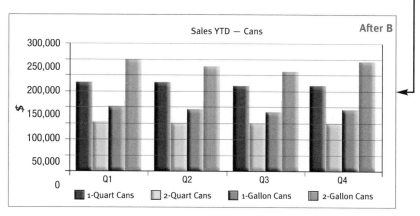

Sales YTD — Cans

After B

■ Each chart/graph should answer the question, "Compared to what?" Time series charts do so by definition, but point-in-time charts need to have the capability to compare to prior periods, control factors for same period, other products, etc. As discussed earlier, we prefer charts to compare current performance to forecast, to keep the emphasis on always looking ahead vs. back (figure 9.9).

FIGURE 9.9 — COMPARED TO WHAT?

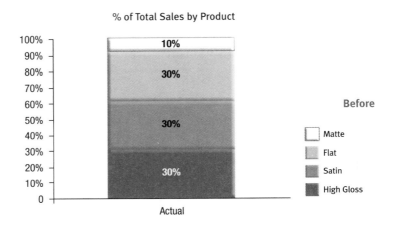

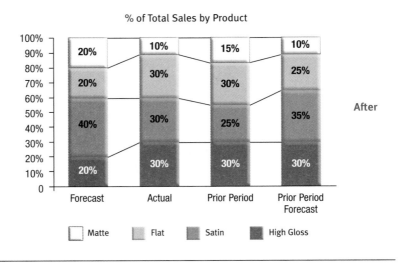

- Always follow the eyes. People read left to right, top to bottom. Design to make that easy and have the most impact.
- Do "main effects" ordering, which means you should present data from highest to lowest or least to most, uniformly increasing or decreasing in size (figure 9.10).

FIGURE 9.10 — MAIN EFFECTS ORDERING

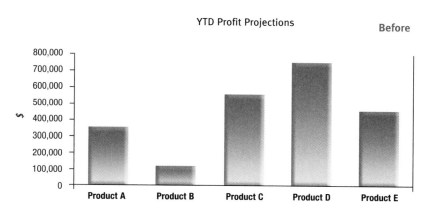

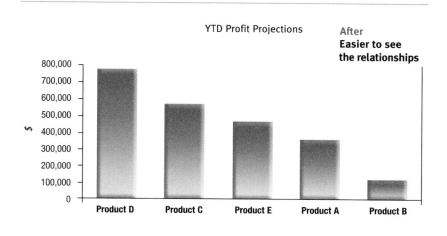

- Avoid using gridlines unless subtle comparisons of elements are required.

- Aspect ratio is the ratio of the height of the graph to the width of the graph. Standard televisions are 4:3 aspect ratio. Widescreens are 5:9. Ideally, use 1:1 when X and Y are measured in the same units. Try to stay within +/-0.25 either way (figure 9.11).

FIGURE 9.11 — PRESENT APPEALING ASPECT RATIOS

Sales by Month
(aspect ratio 1:2.5)

Before

Sales by Month
(aspect ratio 1:1)

After

- Label clearly and comprehensively. Use legends whenever more than one element is depicted in a chart. Each chart should have a title and a timeframe.

- Finally, be, in Einstein's words, "as simple as necessary, and no more."

More Rules of the Road

Now that you're more confident in your knowledge of how to graphically present data more effectively, the following are some of the key considerations for successful dashboard designs that marry multiple graphical elements.

1. **Always consider the audience:** Generally, the more senior the viewer, the higher level the first page summary should be. Also, consider the technical skill of each audience group you have, since that will drive their usage.

2. **Keep your dashboard light, with as few metrics as possible:** Have you ever looked at a chart in a book or newspaper that seemed way too crowded with type or pictures? You probably turned the page, right? Those rules apply here. Less is definitely more. Redundant metrics waste time and therefore lessen the managerial value of the final toolset you create.

3. **Consider a "drill-down" series of dashboards with appropriate variations:** Your CEO, CFO, and other top-level executives probably don't need to see every single dashboard metric you've created in the marketing department. They don't have the time, and you don't want to give anyone an excuse to micromanage. That's why it makes sense to design not just one dashboard, but a series of dashboards with appropriate metrics for different audiences. You're not building a walled system, just a series of nested dashboard pages with "drill-down" capability (see figure 9.12) that can allow anyone to look at the metrics they need at any given point in time. Think of yourself as an editor trying to please various readerships. You may be on the same team, but different executives want different data — give it to them. Also, if you want to keep different groups from trespassing into proprietary data, password-protect various areas of the dashboard to keep eyes where they should be.

FIGURE 9.12 — DASHBOARD DRILL-DOWN SCHEMATIC

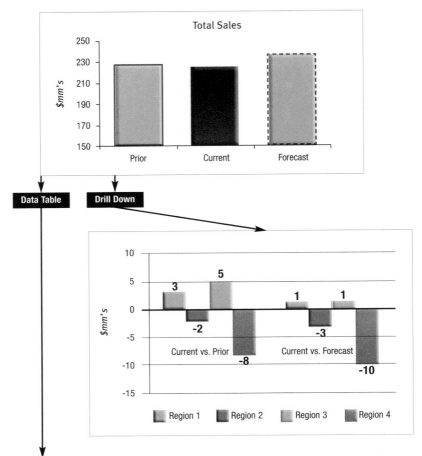

	Prior	Current	Forecast
Region 1	65	68	67
Region 2	34	32	35
Region 3	51	56	55
Region 4	77	69	79
Total Count	**227**	**225**	**236**

	Current vs. Prior	Current vs. Forecast
Region 1	3	1
Region 2	-2	-3
Region 3	5	1
Region 4	-8	-10
Total Country	-2	-11

4. **Look and feel are crucial:** Remember what we said about cognitive load — no more than three to 10 elements per page, and limit the types of graphical devices used in any one page to three. You and your team are best qualified to determine the mix of metrics and how receptive your audience will be to the way you present them. If you do seek outside advice, err on the side of simplicity. As a general rule, changing a two-axis chart to three axes increases the degree of readership difficulty by a factor of 10. Try to live within a two-axis world.

5. **Plan to refresh data on a regular basis:** The frequency with which you refresh the data on your dashboard should correspond to the needs of your business. If things change enough on a day-to-day basis to warrant a reassessment of resource allocation, then it makes sense for the dashboard to be revised daily based on that new data. However, for most companies, even those with real-time sales tracking, business patterns are unlikely to change more often than weekly. For some, it's monthly or quarterly. The people who make day-to-day decisions in a department may need more frequent updates than senior officers of the company. Again, if senior management wants to drill down, they can, but use your resources to update those to whom frequent updates are mission critical. Take the time to plan your dashboard integration with your data warehouse, campaign management tools, marketing enterprise systems, and other software solutions. If you have all of these software solutions working already, you might consider putting your dashboards online, where this information will be more accessible and significantly cheaper to maintain.

6. **Paper or plastic?** We've seen some very sharp and effective marketing dashboards in the form of low-resolution color printouts dropped in people's mailboxes (the real kind, not the "e-kind"). We've also seen some fairly lousy ones presented in some slick and expensive "real-time" online intranets or e-mail links. We can't stress enough that the medium you choose should fit your culture, your need for speed, and your breadth of distribution. If you don't require such frequent updates and your organization's staff is friendlier with paper, by all means, do paper. But if you need to update your dashboard frequently or distribute many versions to many constituents, go electronic. The No. 1 priority is to have

it read and understood by the people making the decisions at all levels. Everything should support that one simple goal.

7. **Roll out:** The well-executed dashboard doesn't require training per se, but as part of the roll-out, it makes sense to have a formal introduction in the style each of your target audiences will receive. Introducing the marketing dashboard may be a good way to spend a little quality time with the board or the executive committee of the company, so don't rule out those opportunities. Making a presentation should be one of your strong points already, so maybe we don't need to say this, but … know your audience and sell it.

8. **Don't fob off this project:** Building an effective marketing dashboard is a lot of work, and it will require continued work and planning once it's launched if it's going to stay effective. It is not a part-time project for the most "get-it-done" person in your department. It is also not something you can delegate to your analytics group. But if you make the effort to do your first marketing dashboard right, particularly with the help of some unbiased external perspective, it will be the most rewarding and effective undertaking you'll experience in your job. It will also build staff morale for a marketing team that currently suffers from lack of attention from senior management.

The most important rule of all? Follow your culture. If it's conservative, design traditionally. If it's innovation-driven, be innovative. If it's technical, be scientific. A dashboard design initiative can be created internally along the guidelines we've suggested, but it never hurts to have additional expert assistance in creating the model that works for you.

CONCLUSION

There are some specific design techniques that facilitate the rapid and accurate absorption of data. These techniques recognize the incredible strengths and inherent limitations of our human visual acuity. But there are some distinct cultural tips to keep in mind when it comes to effective dashboard design. Know your company culture and reflect it in your dashboard design. Know your users and let their needs and preferences dictate your choice of publication medium and update frequency.

With some careful study, even the most complex data can be presented simply and effectively. The key is going beyond your own personal filters of what "looks good" and doing your homework on what is most likely to work for the audience to result in an effective measurement tool.

Sources

1. Kosslyn, S.M., "Graphics and Human Information Processing," *Journal of the American Statistical Association*, 1985.

2. Bacon, Lynd, "Graphical Data Analysis and Visualization Techniques for Marketing Research," AMA Art Forum Proceedings, 1996.

From No-Tech to High-Tech: Selecting the Right Technology Platform to Deliver the Best Dashboard

Now that you know what you want on your dashboard and how to design the graphics, you need to think about the best way to reach your audience. It's time to decide on the right delivery platform.

First and foremost, we'll take this opportunity to state that technology is, after content, a secondary consideration. But it's a close second.

Fact: The slickest dashboard presentation will fail miserably if it is not used by the intended audience as the point of reliance for their decision making. It's equally dangerous to assume that your users will work hard to sort through many pages or screens just to find the one item they want to see most. One need only see how executives respond more enthusiastically and engage more readily with well-designed dashboards to understand the importance of using the right technology to display all the hard work that went into defining the right metrics.

Overall, the appropriate maxim here would likely be, "Use just enough technology to facilitate the key message absorption, and no more."

There are a wide variety of options for dashboard presentation. Choices include:

- paper printouts — a "deck" of color printouts distributed by hand or mail;
- electronic files, circulated by e-mail or posted to a common drive, that are usually a combination of Microsoft's PowerPoint, Excel, and Word;

- intranet browser-based dashboards driven from predefined options embedded in "enterprise" applications such as Oracle/Siebel, SAP, Unica, Aprimo, etc.;
- specialty dashboard design applications that run on the desktop through secure intranet access to one or more data sources; and
- Web-based on-demand dashboard applications accessed through a secure site where Java or Flash pages provide a customized graphics framework calling data from a variety of internal and external sources.

Rather than think of these options as discrete choices, you should consider them as points on a spectrum from manual to automatic, from infrequent to real time, from experimental to permanent, from cheap to, well, less cheap.

Regardless of where you decide to land on the technology spectrum, your objective is to make your dashboards look and work like a good Web site.

The user should intuitively understand the full scope of what she's looking at, and be able to view a single "page" at a time (see the example in figure 10.1 below). Each "page" is a family of related metrics (e.g., brand or customer value or channel) organized in a

FIGURE 10.1 — SAMPLE MARKETING DASHBOARD

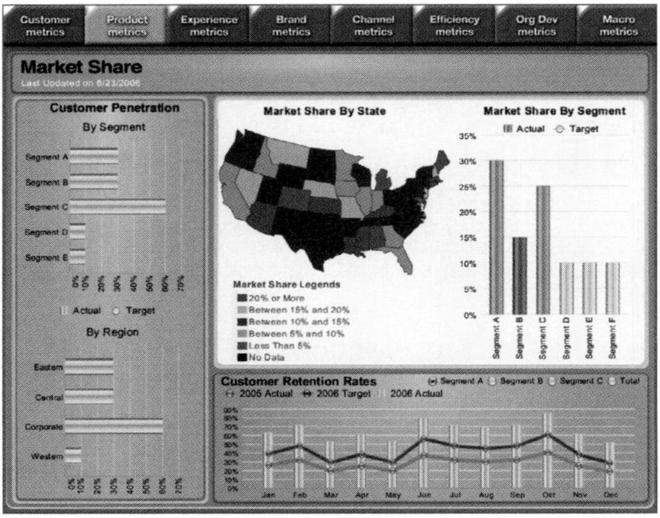

way that tells the story of that area. Her attention can then be choreographed to move fluidly from one page to the next, seeing the full story of performance emerging across family dimensions.

Against this backdrop of seemingly infinite possibilities, we'll attempt to compare and contrast the options using a framework of needs that will guide you to the right solution.

Know What You Need to Measure

By this point in the book, we're hoping you've already decided on a few of the critical metrics for your dashboard. Having put all that effort into the selection process, it makes sense to ensure that metrics are accessible, understood, and easy to absorb and apply.

First and foremost, select a presentation platform that suits the nature of those metrics. Here, timing becomes important. Consider the following:

- Daily sales figures demand an intranet-driven, browser-based platform that allows easy click-throughs for each user's targeted update. Based on the complexity of your organization, you'll need to build in a drill-down feature that will allow access to only relevant figures for specific products, regions, business groups, or all three. The bottom line: It's unlikely that everyone in your organization needs to see the exact same data. As we've stated before, you'll need to do some editing to make sure the right people get the right information.

- Brand performance data is updated less frequently. At most, data from your brand scorecard (see Chapter 6) might refresh monthly. When you do release that portion of your dashboard, shared drive or e-mail circulation might be sufficient. But don't imagine that paper will suffice if your goal is to present a drill down into brand perceptions by segment, geography, or constituency group.

- Staff skill development metrics might only be assessed quarterly and paper reports might be just fine. In fact, eyes-only paper or password-protected computer updates might be preferable if you're providing data on specific individuals or departments below the summary level. Consider privacy issues when appropriate and match the delivery system accordingly. That's particularly important whenever you're talking about staff or individual performance.

But what if you want to report all three?

Selecting the presentation platform for your dashboard should always adhere to a simple rule: Follow the leader. The critical metrics requiring the most frequently refreshed, most dissectible reporting structures should be the ones that determine your choice of platform.

Remember, your goal is to immediately engage your audience to dive into the dashboard to uncover insights. So the platform must fit the information you're trying to share. A dashboard that presents quarterly summaries when decisions are made monthly is not likely to be perceived as being very relevant, regardless of how good it looks. Unless the information is more timely than other sources they use, your dashboard will not be seen as a relevant, helpful tool.

Understand the Needs of Your Audience

Successful dashboards are designed to meet the needs of their primary customers: the executives who use them. Consequently, those creating the dashboard should take into account the information absorption preferences and habits of the intended audience to the greatest extent possible. Before design, there needs to be an understanding of how key groups prefer to receive information.

A little ethnography might help here. Talk to the intended senior recipients. While you're asking them what they would like to see measured and what they regularly refer to now, ask them to show you. Observe the way they retrieve the information to share with you. Do they dig into their shoulder bag or briefcase to pull out a file and hand you some printouts from an e-mail attachment? Do they turn to their computers? If so, do they fumble around a bit to find the right file in the right folder or are they fairly quick to open or launch the application they're looking for? Was it on their "desktop" or nested in a menu of folders?

Watching the habits of your target audience can provide many clues to the right presentation platform. But don't assume their past habits restrict their ability to adapt to new delivery vehicles. Even those with a historical preference for printed sales reports may respond very positively to new electronic delivery platforms that give them faster access to more information. You clearly don't want to let the current habits solely dictate your dashboard technology solution.

But you also don't want to introduce new layers of technology without thoroughly testing the receptivity of the key constituents to ensure they see it as beneficial, and not just complicating.

This is a crucial point. You *will* be forced to make tradeoffs in your dashboard presentation platform. Count on it. Be alert to identifying your degrees of freedom in the early stages of exploration so you increase the size of the ultimate solution set from which to choose.

The bottom line: If the key executive users find the dashboard confusing or complicated to use, they will revert to their familiar reports and you'll lose the opportunity to get everyone working off the same page. It doesn't matter if you've painstakingly selected just the right metrics and had the key stakeholders embrace them; complexity in execution wipes out all good work that went before it.

The Need for Summary Insights vs. Data Mining

How far are you planning to let your audience drill down in your dashboard? One layer? Two? Five?

If your dashboard is forecasting sales as a function of brand preference, you might want users to drill down to a regional or product-line view. From there, you might want them to drill across to see a view by customer value segment. But do they really need to drill into a view by a time-series migration of segments, or to a view that shows them individual customer survey responses compared to transactions?

Data mining can become a real danger in the wrong hands. Sure, it might be very convenient for the EVP of sales to be able to drill into a time-series analysis of coffee breaks by redheaded sales reps making over $100,000. But do they have a true need to drill in so deep, or is that something better left to others who have more expertise in query construction and interpretation of data? What makes this difficult is that if you ask them, they'll tell you they want more data. That's just human nature.

However, if you accept that the purpose of a marketing dashboard is as an executive information tool that puts critical insights at the user's disposal with minimum effort and time, then you realize that drilling down more than two levels is really turning the system into a business intelligence tool. And that's where big complexities creep in. So instead of asking the executives if they want access to more information at their fingertips, pose the question in a way that underscores the tradeoffs between more information and simplicity of use. Then see what answer you get.

If you still plan to install a significant amount of drill-down or drill-across capability, your choices for a dashboard platform become increasingly linked to your underlying data collection and aggregation needs. Microsoft Excel will likely perform too slowly if you're using tables consisting of tens of thousands of rows of data. OLAP cubes or large relational databases require more facile database software.

If you already have one of these datamart applications installed and are considering adding the dashboard capabilities on top of it, great — assuming, of course, that your datamart includes *all* the data to support *all* your critical metrics, or can easily be configured to do so. If not, what benefit do you really get by tying your dashboard to it? At best you'll have terrific data for some of your critical metrics, but an overall ineffective dashboard with big gaps in telling the whole story.

There's really no justification for buying a datamart/data-mining application just to run a marketing dashboard. Today's dashboard applications are plenty powerful at pulling data from multiple sources, eliminating the need to have all data integrated into a single data structure. You can always consider a more complex solution later, but you don't need to start there unless you're sure you know exactly where you want your dashboard system to begin and what path it will take in evolving over time.

Remember to keep your key information objectives close at hand when selecting your platform and don't be afraid to put a stop to "nice-to-have" drill-down provisions to preserve simplicity and ease of use of the "need-to-haves."

Prototype, Prototype, Prototype

Let's assume for the moment that you are reading this book because you are attempting to develop your organization's first marketing dashboard.

Let's further assume that, as with most complex undertakings involving many people and processes, it might not be exactly right after the first pass. It would be a shame to invest a great deal of money buying, installing, and programming an expensive data presentation system only to discover later that you didn't need that Cadillac system and, worse, that it didn't support some unique dashboard needs after the first release. So many organizations fall into the trap of letting the system functionality dictate the dashboard design while forgetting how necessary it is to have buy-in with key decision makers.

Paradoxically, it can be helpful in some situations to begin with a dashboard platform that *isn't* part of an integrated datamart solution, but rather draws data from the many current independent sources you have in place today. This approach lets users experience the dashboard interface the way you think it should work, and then channel their feedback to define the eventual requirements for a more structured datamart. This approach could save you tens or hundreds of thousands of dollars in data integration costs in the long run.

Even if you already have an enterprise system installed in your company like Siebel or SAP, you might want to consider developing your first iterations of the dashboard with PowerPoint, Excel, or Flash just to find the right blend of graphic presentation, drill-down relationships, and overall usability. Once you're confident you have the fundamentals right, you can upgrade your enterprise system license to incorporate their dashboard modules and synch both data and presentation up to a single application engine.

Platform Technology — A Closer Look

Now that you've defined the basic needs of your dashboard system, you'll probably want more detail on the types of technology solutions available to make your goals happen. Some are better performers than others.

Desktop Solutions

The desktop applications of PowerPoint and Excel are inexpensive and very flexible. They have far more flexibility than most people ever use. You can use PowerPoint to design an almost limitless graphic presentation layer with navigation buttons to move around in a non-linear fashion. You can use it to "call" Excel graphs, charts, or tables as required.

Older versions of Excel (including 2003 or XP) have restrictions on the amount of data you can hold in any one spreadsheet and data structures that aren't optimized for fast performance. That's why your screen flickers when you import or refresh Excel charts called from another program. This is especially problematic if you're trying to call data into a chart in real time. However, for the vast majority of basic data summary and storage, Excel can be perfectly acceptable. The big advantage to using these popular desktop tools is that almost everyone has familiarity with them and users won't need a lot of training. In fact, most people use only a small fraction of the capabilities of PowerPoint or Excel. Also, if the person who designed your dashboard moves on, it won't be hard to get someone with skills to fill the role.

The biggest limitation to the Office desktop tools is the inability to target relevant information to individual users with different needs. Your options are usually limited to setting up one huge master file that everyone needs to wade through to find what they're specifically interested in seeing, or creating and managing dozens of smaller files and custom distribution lists – a recipe for error if there ever was one.

Desktop Add-Ons

If there's a limit to Excel and Powerpoint, it's in the number of ways you can present graphical presentations easily. While they're both extremely flexible, getting the most out of them can involve some pretty elaborate gymnastics not described in the basic user manuals.

To extend the capabilities of these applications, several aftermarket players have launched data visualization tools that work on top of Excel. These are relatively easy to use and work with the desktop standards to extend your range of options and enhance the user experience.

Crystal Xcelsius™ is a tool marketed by Business Objects that provides a menu of standard chart formats not found in Excel like dials, gauges, slide rules, maps, and combinations of bar/line/area graphs that Excel doesn't support.

Chart FX® is another solution in the same genre. Either package sits on your desktop and calls up Excel data tables that you can customize graphically. You can modify the attributes of each basic chart type, export them separately, or place them on a complete dashboard page before exporting them into PowerPoint. You can even create data selection filters and simple navigation structures.

FIGURE 10.2 — CRYSTAL XCELSIUS™ SAMPLE CHARTS

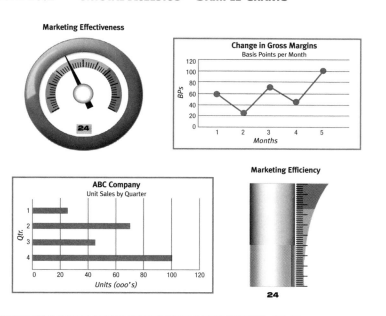

Both applications also allow you to import and export data and your graphics in XML format into Web-page templates if you are presenting on your intranet.

These applications typically cost several hundred dollars per user but don't require any software for your dashboard viewer if you are exporting to PowerPoint or Flash for browser-based access.

Unfortunately, neither option solves the problem of user-customization mentioned earlier. They both create single-viewer files where anyone with access sees the same data. So if you're anticipating the need to separate users into classes or categories (for example, "insiders" vs. "non-insiders"), you need to build and maintain multiple dashboards — one for each user group. That can get both complex and expensive.

And while this class of tools can make native Excel graphs look like antiques from a management museum, they still have some formidable limitations. If, for example, you want users to dynamically filter the slice of data they see by more than one dimension at a time (e.g., by region *and* by market segment), these tools will frustrate you.

In the end, these are terrific tools for dramatically improving the presentation of everyday chart structures. But it's this simplicity that makes you want to believe they are capable of so much more. In the end, the love for the tools proves unrequited. You get what you pay for.

Campaign Management and Marketing Resource Management Tools

Software applications used by marketers to manage large numbers of initiatives and track expenditures are terrific for reporting graphically on the response to those campaigns and summarizing the spend patterns. But, generally, they work off of a closed data model for efficiency. That means that applications like Epiphany, Unica, Aprimo, and others in this class have a proprietary (and highly structured) database model underneath their screens and functions. These structured data models can make it difficult to import some types of data that don't fit the predetermined setup. For example, customer transactional data would import just fine, but brand preference data from surveys might not fit as easily into a campaign management tool, nor would HR tables summarizing staff certification levels.

As a general rule, campaign management tools are not effective as primary dashboard platforms unless you're a direct response marketing company looking for your marketing dashboard to focus solely on campaign metrics often associated with direct response tools and channels. Their reporting and charting capabilities are improving rapidly, but they were never intended to be the repository of everything you would likely need to deploy a comprehensive dashboard.

Enterprise BI Applications

Slowly but surely, enterprise applications like those from SAP and Oracle and business intelligence solutions from Hyperion, Cognos, and MicroStrategies are enhancing their marketing functionality to automate the marketing functions of resource allocation, optimization, and correlation with business results. They also have the advantage of often being integrated with sales pipelines, CRM systems, and customer service platforms that provide a richer view of the impact of marketing investments on those critical stages of the buying cycles.

Enterprise applications also have the advantage of increasingly being open data structures. They are built on a three-level architecture that separates the "presentation layer" (or how the graphics or tables are displayed) from the "logic layer" (which parameterizes how data elements relate to one another) from the "data layer" (where data of any type can be imported into the system). You can have your enterprise application calling data from multiple other files or servers at any time, always presenting the most current information. If you need HR data, you program the application to get it from the HR server. If you need sales data, you get it from the data warehouse. If you need research survey data, you can pull it directly from your vendor's secure site.

Of course, all this data integration comes at a pretty stiff price both in terms of the software license fees and the labor required to standardize all the data elements into forms it can work with. In general, you can expect to pay several hundred thousand dollars in license fees, plus at least that much for the installation, data integration, and configuration. In addition, you also have user and administrator training costs, which can easily run upwards of a few thousand dollars per trainee. So before you know it, you can spend $1 million-plus to install one of these systems. The biggest companies often spend $10 million or more for complete integration and training of hundreds of marketing and sales users.

While the major players are making good strides in improving their graphical dashboard capabilities, their current offerings are suitable for most needs, if a bit uninspired. They're also not all that easy to configure or simple to change, so you can't quickly evolve your dashboard to the most effective, efficient structure for your organization's needs. And if you operate in a very dynamic environment where things change frequently and quickly, this may just be a critical flaw.

The most successful instances of enterprise applications driving dashboard development are characterized by a few common traits:

■ They don't attempt to customize too much too fast, working instead within the "off-the-shelf" capabilities of the software while more detailed requirements are defined.

■ They institute a comprehensive change-management process that takes into account all the different ways your business processes will have to change to accommodate the new system.

■ They don't skimp on the training. If the users feel stupid interacting with the system, they won't use the dashboard.

And finally, successful enterprise application implementations pay close attention to the initial data integration to ensure data collection processes that lead to high data integrity, avoiding the risk of importing "garbage-in, gospel-out" syndrome.

Dashboard Specialty Tools

There is one additional class of dashboard tools worthy of consideration. These are characterized by highly flexible and visually engaging user interfaces that are custom-assembled for your specific charting needs and sit atop any combination of data sources. Two are worthy of mention here.

CORDA's CenterView™ platform uses Java-coded graphical objects drawing data from multiple sources to assemble a streamlined dashboard structure where each chart object can be dragged and dropped onto any page view. You can create virtually any type of chart object and create any number of filtering mechanisms. And CORDA permits integration to single-source log-on networks so user permissions established for corporate security purposes can be seamlessly used to channel relevant information directly to those who want/need it most.

The CenterView™ application can be licensed to run on your intranet servers at a cost ranging from $20,000 to $200,000 or more, depending upon the number of licensed users. Then you still have

FIGURE 10.3 — SAMPLE DASHBOARD IN VFX PLATFORM™

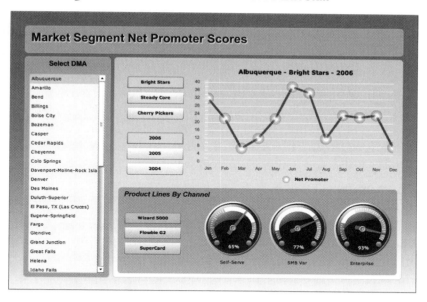

to create your own page views. Here too, however, the flexibility to create anything you may want comes with a price payable in complexity. Learning to use the platform and its myriad options for configuration and design requires both a strong technical acumen and many days of training to take best advantage of all the capabilities.

From a totally different direction, The Dashboard Company recently introduced the VFX Platform™: an on-demand dashboard tool that operates over the Internet while allowing all the data to stay secure behind your firewall. Its trick is creating individual dashboard page views as Flash files, thereby separating the chart from the underlying data until it is launched in the user's browser. Because the page views can be developed in Flash or in Flex, Adobe's latest object-oriented graphical programming language, they are limitless in flexibility and visually stunning. And VFX uses a unique method of ensuring user relevancy through creation of "perspectives" — different views into the dashboard — which can be assigned to individual users to control or streamline who sees what data.

This option is very appropriate for those companies seeking an outsourced solution, letting programmers assemble the components from your direction and manage the hosted application on your behalf. The VFX Platform™ costs between $3,000 and $15,000 per month (which includes all hosting, training, and maintenance), depending upon the number of registered users. Page views developed by programmers typically cost in the range of $2,000 to $12,000 apiece, depending upon complexity.

Both of these platforms are on the leading edge of dashboard construction and management, and are worthy of exploration before deciding on your final choice — even if you already have a business intelligence datamart on-site.

CONCLUSION

There are many options for choosing a dashboard technology platform, ranging from mostly manual to fully automated; from limited to infinitely flexible; from do-it-yourself to do-it-for-you; and from low-cost to high-priced. Regardless of which technology platform you choose for your dashboard installation, your probability of success is highly correlated to the quality of your change-management process. Getting the entire marketing organization to align on a common lexicon, need set, and desired experience can be a daunting task that is best approached in a highly inclusive, consensus-building manner.

If you use the criteria laid out in this chapter to assess your options and stick to these simple principles, your dashboard platform will enhance the intended effect, not obscure or obstruct it.

SOURCES

CenterView is a trademark of CORDA Technologies, Inc.

Chart FX is a registered trademark of Software FX, Inc.

Crystal Xcelsius is a trademark of Business Objects, Inc.

VFX Platform is a trademark of The Dashboard Company LLC.

The Role of the Dashboard in the Evolution of the Marketing Organization

T he marketing dashboard is more than just a way to measure the effectiveness of your marketing expenditures. It's a means of conceiving, structuring, and monitoring any level of organizational change you seek to make in your marketing organization.

By viewing your dashboard broadly, you can use the development process to bring great clarity to the current and future roles of marketing in your company, the gaps between them, and the key milestones for closing those gaps. Your dashboard can become more than just a leading indicator of financial and strategic success. It can be a beacon of organizational leadership effectiveness and a model for others in the company to follow to promote cross-functional collaboration and achieve a higher level of efficiency — all of which are sure to make the marketing expenditures immeasurably more successful.

Through strategy mapping, resource mapping, defining the specific role of marketing, and developing hypotheses on critical leading indicator metrics, you can't help but put the emphasis on finding the places where current organizational structures, culture, and processes inhibit effective measurement. In other words, you will find the enemy of integrated measurement is not in the finance or sales department, but more likely in the mirror.

Effective marketing measurement on a strategic (vs. tactical) level is undermined by seven common organizational mistakes. See which ones pertain to you.

1. Setting performance metrics beyond the span of control: Keeping everyone's eye on the bottom line is good. Linking too much of their bonus or merit consideration to key

performance indicators based on financial outcomes too far removed from marketing influence isn't. It often results in a demoralized marketing team that is resentful of other functional departments and less likely to seek input or build consensus when it comes to strategy development, program execution, or measurement.

2. **Letting the metrics become the objectives:** One of the big automotive components suppliers challenged its team to build a car-door hinge system that was significantly more smooth and quiet than the current approach. They succeeded. But, the cost per door tripled. If you've hired smart people, be careful how you state their objectives. They will find a way to achieve them.

3. **Impeding the flow of bad news:** Metrics in marketing won't work unless they promote objectivity — which means accepting the bad with the good. Equating reward solely with success sends the clear signal that being the messenger is a good way to get shot unless all the news is good. Find subtle ways to reward truth along with success, and link the two together in the minds of your team.

4. **Delegating measurement strategy:** In selecting the right marketing metrics, the decision maker has to have not only a big-picture perspective, but the clout to negotiate marketing's new science with the rest of the organization.[1] Mid-level managers can't do this. Only a person at the top can assess how much change marketing can take in one step and in which direction the group must move. Plus, when measurement strategy is delegated, truth and insight often take a back seat to rationalization and justification. Measurement requires leadership that ensures that every person in the organization is focused on being creative, being supportive, taking initiative, and performing as a team player. Appointing a trusted staff member to be the chief of the measurement police is a sure way to cut them out of the informal communications channels where the real information is shared. You may decide to have someone coordinate the process, but the actual measurement (and results) should be owned by a broad group of marketing leaders, chief among them the CMO.

5. **Allowing IT to control the agenda:** In an increasingly data-driven marketing era, IT is responsible for collecting and storing data, mining customer transaction files, and sending and receiving messages in record time. Consequently the path to progress in marketing measurement is often dependent upon the same time- and resource-starved IT people who support all the other mission-critical company functions. But the prioritization of those IT resources is most often made with an eye toward fixing holes in cash-flow management or operations support, not marketing process improvement. Consequently, marketing must be prepared to present its case by simultaneously forecasting the business value of the proposed changes *and* the cost of outsourcing the work. In larger marketing organizations, it often makes sense to have an IT liaison on the marketing team whose responsibility includes the mid- and long-range planning of company IT capabilities to support marketing evolution and to translate the inevitable "we can't do that" IT response into creative solutions for progress.

6. **Neglecting to give researchers and analysts respect:** When was the last time you met a CMO who rose up through research? Researchers and analysts typically live at the lower end of the marketing pay scales and often have no career path. They need to act as thought leaders within the organization, leveraging the thought and data models they build in marketing and in all of the business functions it touches. When researchers rise as thought leaders, they encourage the use of facts and data to make smart decisions. So the smart CMO will see that these people get the training in communications skills and leadership development to expose their talents more broadly and spread that discipline within the department. It's time to rethink the role of research and decision analytics in our marketing structures, not just expand on the same old models.

7. **Forgetting about training in measurement:** And we wonder why we hear so much complaining about skill shortages. Survey after survey on improving marketing measurement cites the No. 1 CMO need as "getting the right skills in place." But by our observation, fewer than one in 10 mid-to-large-sized marketing departments have comprehensive skill-building programs in place.

Each and every one of these common symptoms is sufficient to block progress in achieving measurement synthesis horizontally across the marketing organization. Only when we start breaking down these barriers will we begin to see the "big picture" of marketing performance in the context of the whole company's continuous improvement plan.

The process of developing a comprehensive marketing dashboard is intended to focus the marketing organization on setting the right objectives and choosing the best metrics to help minimize the risks inherent in some of the specific challenges above. The dashboard helps create a framework for defining what success looks like, clarifying the roles and responsibilities of the contributing players, and then stimulating the dialogue around how the marketing organization should be structured to achieve it.

So with regards to marketing organizational development, the best dashboard is one that places structured emphasis on measuring the right "big things" to guide the marketing department towards its mission(s), without stifling it under a "tyranny of a hundred metrics."

But where is the balance between structured measurement and a culture of creativity? How do you set the boundaries without dampening the spirit of innovation so critical to marketing success?

The Paradox of Standards

Thomas W. Malone, professor of management at MIT's Sloan School of Management, has spent the better part of a long academic career researching organizational effectiveness. In his book, *The Future of Work: How the New Order of Business Will Shape Your Organization, Your Management Style, and Your Life,* Malone points to a "paradox of standards."[2] He says clearly and firmly defining a few rules (controls) in the most risky areas of the organization sets creativity free in all others.

For example, eBay doesn't "control" much of what happens on its vast global network. It allows buyers and sellers to interact as they will. What makes the network so successful is the clear framework of rules (the exclusion of certain product categories and bidding processes, for example) that are just firm enough to protect the interests of the greater good and no more restrictive. Certainly no one would accuse eBay of stifling creativity that inhibits growth.

Marketers have long understood this paradox in key efforts like ad copy briefs. Decades of experience have shown that the best creative briefs focus succinctly on a distinct business objective and impose as few firm parameters as possible, but do include some. The creatives must work within the parameters to find new dimensions of communications effectiveness that achieve the business goal. Apply too many parameters, and you'll get boring, uninspired copy unlikely to accomplish its mission of persuasion. Define too few, and the ads diverge from the strategy, unlikely to create the desired attitudinal or behavioral shifts.

This is how Malone's "paradox" works. The better defined the playing field is, the more likely the result will be a win. Finding the right balance between objective definition and subjective interpretation is the difference between winning and losing.

But achieving this balance is certainly not easy in the explosive complexity of today's marketing organization. Several companies who have made good progress report that their success came from evolving from a command-and-control structure to one focused on defining the right set of controls and then applying all energies to drawing the best out of more autonomous, decentralized operating groups.

Applying a Flexible Framework

McDonald's has employed a "flexible framework" to deal with the hundreds of customer segments it serves worldwide, across dozens of cultures. To rebuild its brand relevancy after several years of sales attrition, McDonald's required that communications be open, honest, and fully transparent while speaking in the consumer's own voice. Beyond that, McDonald's sets firm expectations for business outcomes and lets the creative process interpret the brand in each culture in ways most appealing to the local customer.

CMO VIEW: FLEXIBLE FRAMEWORK FOR SUCCESS

Larry Light
CHIEF MARKETING OFFICER
McDonald's Corporation

"We built a plan to win around seven principles we called the Seven P's. The Seven P's were: promise, people, products, place, price, promotion, and performance. The promise P is top management's responsibility; it defines the direction of the brand. The performance P is where the metrics take place. The five P's in the middle are actions we take. The performance P is the result. For each of the action P's we have measures, and then we have some aggregate measures across them. Let's take the people P, for example. Two of the metrics are 'employer reputation' and 'employee pride.' So we have both an external measure — reputation as an employer — and an internal measure — pride. We believe that our brand image, our marketing, and our PR all affect our reputation and the pride of our employees."[3]

Lest you believe for a minute that the inmates have been left to run the asylum, be assured that McDonald's diligently measures the evolution in its brand equity around the world and correlates it closely to sales and transactional behavior. The framework says that marketing initiatives must be successful at generating substantial payback in the form of in-store profits. That ultimate accountability causes regional McDonald's marketers and agencies to think two, three, or four times about improving the expected return before they exercise their autonomy.

Here's a quick test of your own organization's posture vis-à-vis a "flexible framework": Are your current brand compliance standards dictated in excruciating detail in an effort to "control" rogue users, or articulated in a manner that speaks less to logo size and color than to the desired impact on message recipients and their perceptions?

The marketing dashboard is, in essence, your own "flexible framework." You'll probably develop it in stages, starting with too many metrics as a result of uncertainty about the real drivers, then peeling back layers of parameters selectively as you validate the things that are truly (predictively) correlated with success, and allowing the organization time to acclimate to its new freedoms. A good starting point is to look at the regular reporting requirements imposed on your staff and seek to turn the focus from activity-oriented metrics (what did you *do* last week?) to results-oriented ones (what did you *accomplish* last week?). From there, you can work with each subgroup to map out key initiatives and ensure alignment with your broader objectives. Then keep asking the question, "How do we forecast success, and which of our metrics are the true leading indicators?"

Once people understand how their work will be evaluated and their results monitored, creativity and autonomy can thrive in a more productive manner.

Dashboards and the Integrated Marketing Organization

When they see the word "integrated," most marketers think "communications." They envision public relations, advertising, direct marketing, and promotions all working together harmoniously to deliver a concerted message across channels. That's the '90s definition.

In this limited-but-still-common structure, marketing has a box on the org chart reporting to the CEO. Implicit in the functions of that box are the usual marketing responsibilities like advertising, promotions, sponsorships, trade shows, direct, and database management — all the traditional elements of managing the brand.

Communications programs are managed for ROI against benchmarks. Media-mix models may be employed to maximize efficiency of advertising dollars, and brand equities may be tracked to gauge progress at favorably influencing perceptions.

Chances are that few, if any, of these measures get much play outside the marketing department. Yet each year marketing budgets reflect the desire of the rest of the company to minimize marketing waste.

The new meaning of "fully integrated" for the marketing department is one that places the emphasis on active collaboration with most, if not all, other departments in the company to improve the appeal, volume, and profitability of the company's products or services to achieve the maximum value from each customer relationship. A quick glance at the chart in figure 11.1 will tell you how your marketing department stands with respect to other roles in the fully integrated organization.

FIGURE 11.1 — THE MANY ROLES OF THE INTEGRATED MARKETING ORGANIZATION

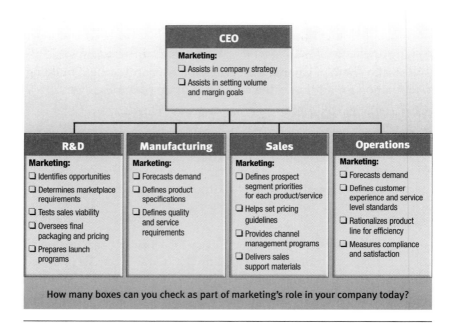

The fully integrated marketing department of today manages the brand on a much more expansive level, taking a clear role in defining and handling many aspects of the customer value proposition from product or service conception to forecasting to sales effectiveness to touchpoint experience. The fully integrated marketing department is much more likely to be linked closely with the overall organizational planning process, in many instances helping to set the strategic agenda for the entire company and establishing key cross-functional milestones like customer satisfaction, share-of-customer penetration, and perceptions of quality. It is more likely to be speaking the same language as the rest of the organization — revenues, operating margins, efficiencies, and process improvement. And the budgeting process for the fully integrated marketing department uses the company's overall sales and strategic goals as an input variable, not an afterthought.

For those of you thinking, "Yeah, I'd like to get my marketing organization more integrated with the rest of the company and stop being the kid with the nose pressed up against the candy-store window," be warned: Many marketing careers have been ruined when ambition and a sense of entitlement outstripped organizational ability.

Successfully integrating marketing into other parts of the organization often is not something for which other functional department heads are clamoring. It might not even be on the CEO's list of good things to do this year. You may need to commit yourself to a slow, steady, and stealthy path of gaining the permission to contribute and building a reputation for adding value without usurping control … which is exactly where your marketing dashboard comes in.

By promoting a cross-functional approach to developing your dashboard, you demonstrate the desires to be both objective and accountable in measuring marketing performance, as well as the leadership skills to reach out to groups with whom you might historically have been in conflict. Requesting (and respecting) their perspectives in how to define and measure marketing success can illuminate the areas where your peers take a different view of the role of marketing and facilitate the dialogue necessary to bridge the gaps, or at least begin the healing.

In short, the process of developing and implementing your dashboard can be the perfect "cover" for redefining the role of marketing in the broader organizational context and further integrating marketing into the core of the business operation.

Setting the Course for Change Management

By now you see the potential for a marketing dashboard to be more than just a way to measure marketing effectiveness — much more. Done properly, a dashboard is a roadmap for change in the marketing organization. But like any roadmap, its usefulness is dependent upon knowing where you are starting from and where you are going.

Defining those two points on the map can be challenging. One is all about vision; conceiving and articulating a destination that achieves ambitious goals for the evolution of marketing over a three-to-five-year period. The other is about honesty; realistically and objectively assessing where your present organization is on the key dimensions of success required to fulfill the vision.

Most companies find it easier to dive into the assessment than the vision. It's much easier for people to look around at the way things are and identify the flaws they perceive inhibit progress. It also promotes action in the spirit of "getting something done instead of sitting around contemplating our bellybuttons."

Unfortunately, therein lies the trap.

Starting with the assessment almost always results in failure to achieve the goals for two primary reasons.

First, the assessment process often colors the outcome from the start. It's much the same as the "uncertainty principle" in physics, where attempting to measure the precise speed or location of a subatomic particle results in changing the fundamental characteristics one is trying to measure. Natural human behavior is to approach the marketing measurement challenge as "problem/solution." First we define the problem, then we prescribe the solution. But when our "problem" is defined by the limitations of the current world view, we are destined to set the wrong framework for success, and much more likely to measure not what really *is*, but what we *think* is.

Second, allocating our precious human and financial capital to fixing today's problems makes us feel better about going home at night having "done something," but it dramatically reduces our bandwidth for achieving breakthrough change. Not to suggest that we ignore the things that are broken and in need of fixing. In many instances, failure to fix today's problems will preclude even having a tomorrow to worry about. But unless you're in one of those dire situations, you need to weigh the expected value of the fix against the opportunity cost of allocating the resources to cracking the code on the bigger, really tough problems that fundamentally impinge on our prospects for growth.

For these reasons, starting with the assessment is unlikely to lead to much more than incrementalism in compensating for the inherent structural flaws.

By starting with the definition of the objective — the vision — we are taking on a much greater challenge, but one potentially more worthy of conquering with respect to the expected value of success.

Tackling the vision means defining, in specific terms, what we want marketing effectiveness to look like at a given point in time down the road. I say a "given point in time" because we do not yet want to put a stake in the calendar until we know what we're up against. Establishing artificial 12-, 24-, or 36-month goals in the mistaken belief that "we have plenty of time to figure out how to get there" is one of the most common forms of organizational derailment known to management consultants in all industries.

Rather, we want to define the vision first in terms of the following dimensions:

1. What is the definition of "success" for marketing?

2. What should be the process for allocating marketing resources to achieve the greatest practical degree of confidence in the expected return?

3. What critical business processes need to be in place to facilitate 1 and 2 above?

4. What organizational structure will best position us to deliver on that definition of success?

5. What skills will be required?

6. What tools will be necessary?

7. What is the right incentive structure to ensure marketing personnel are motivated to achieve high levels of performance?

The answers to these questions become the "goal states" on each of the seven dimensions.

For each dimension, we then work backwards to identify the major prerequisites of progress that need to be achieved prior to obtaining the goal. These are the "milestones" that mark our progress towards goals over time. Some dimensions may have few milestones, others may have many. When we lay them out in a "success map" form like the one shown in figure 11.2, the goal state is on the right, the current state is on the left, and the milestones (denoted by 1/1, 3/2, etc.) are indicated on each dimension.

FIGURE 11.2 — SUCCESS MAP TO 5-YEAR GOALS

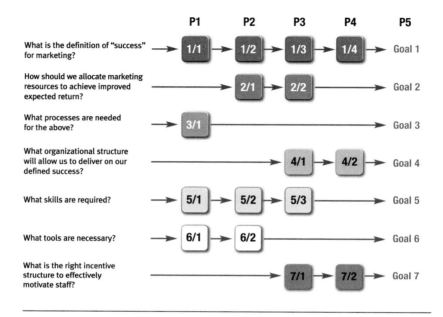

With this success map, we can now more intelligently identify the timeframes required to achieve key milestones (and the overall goals) in the context of variables such as:

■ the organization's ability to take on more change quickly;

■ the presence of necessary leaders to spearhead the change;

■ the competitive realities of having to "build the plane while flying it"; and

■ the ability to smooth the flow of any restructuring expenses.

By assigning timeframes to each milestone, we now have all the necessary components to measure organizational evolution on our marketing dashboard. Our dashboard is now no longer just a read on the past and future effectiveness of marketing expenditures, it is a roadmap for the evolution of the marketing organization.

Whose Job Is It?

Who should develop and maintain the dashboard? Is it the CMO? The SVP research? VP of marketing intelligence? Of course, the right

answer depends a great deal on your current organizational structure and culture. However, there are a few guidelines to help make
the decision.

First, if you want your dashboard to be used by everyone in the
department, you need to make everyone feel like they own it. That
means that the process you go through to define what is on your
dashboard and how it gets implemented should be a very participa-
tive one driven by the direction of the CMO but involving at least
the 10% or so of most influential marketing staffers from across
disciplines. If you are organized by product or segment lines, then
each major product or segment group should be represented. If you
are functionally structured, then research, analytics, brand development,
promotions, and marketing operations should all be active stakeholders in the process.

Second, it often makes sense to have a single individual be responsible
for achieving each phase of the dashboard implementation plan,
but not necessarily the same individual for each phase. Consider
pairing one of your stronger conceptualizers with one of your best
team-builders in the early stages of alignment and definition of key
metrics. Then pass the baton to someone more steeped in process
management and practical problem solving for the initial implementation stages. And for the validation stage, look to your most analytical
resource who's most likely to be completely objective in their assessments and gain the trust of the rest of the group.

Once your dashboard is up and running, its content evolution
should be directed by a steering committee of key users, perhaps
rotating among various groups annually to keep the size of the
group smaller than 10. The technical operation (data integrity,
intranet accessibility, password maintenance, etc.) is best placed in
the hands of a marketing operations person.

Like most change processes, the design and implementation process is
highly dependent upon involving the right people in the right roles.
Tim Ambler from London Business School has a wonderfully simple
way of categorizing those likely to help from those likely to hinder
the progress — as shown in figure 11.3.

FIGURE 11.3 — CATEGORIES OF EMPLOYEE BUY-IN

UNDERSTANDING	COMMITMENT	
	Low	High
High	Bystanders	Champions
Low	Weak Links	Loose Cannons

From *Marketing and the Bottom Line* by Tim Ambler, Financial Times Prentice Hall.[4]

Finding your "champions" to lead the initial change process is, predictably, very important. The real success however comes when you have convinced the "bystanders" to get committed and bring their expertise to the process. Then you can focus on using your dashboard to keep the "loose cannons" in line.

Training and Application

Once your dashboard has been designed and implemented, you may be faced with training dozens, hundreds, or even thousands of users across dozens of languages and cultures. In our experience, the larger the challenge, the greater the need for external help.

If you're training 12 marketing people all based in the U.S. on how to use your new dashboard, chances are it is not so complex that you can't accomplish many of your goals in a few brief meetings in which people are brought to the same room (real or virtual) and walked through the use of the dashboard by one of the implementation team members.

But if you're rolling your dashboard out to a few hundred people across six or more time zones, then you will likely benefit from the help of a professional training organization. In our experience, bringing in professional trainers and asking them to help construct effective learning modules given your training challenge results in a higher adoption rate than DIY efforts for three reasons:

- Outsiders are focused on the human learning challenge, not on the "logic" of what you've built.

- Outsiders are more attuned to subtle "rejection" risks and thus more likely to catch critical flaws early and correct for them faster.

- The use of outside trainers tends to send the message that the company is serious about employees needing to learn this and dedicated to helping even the most intimidated staff members become proficient in something new.

Finally, if the measure of dashboard effectiveness is the degree to which it noticeably informs and speeds decision making, then the decision process itself needs to be modified to promote dashboard adoption. For example, including a standard question in the beginning of each meeting (once the key question for resolution has been identified) along the lines of "what do we know?" will remind participants of the importance of monitoring the dashboard for insight into what's worked, working, and likely to work looking forward. It also has the positive side effect of identifying knowledge gaps that the dashboard might be adapted to close.

The burden for this organizational adoption falls squarely on the shoulders of the CMO and her key lieutenants to inculcate the culture with the right questions. After all, if the CMO isn't visibly interested in keeping dashboard insights close at hand, why would anyone else in the department be?

CMO View: Earning Trust with the Board

Rob Malcolm
President of Marketing, Sales, and Innovation
Diageo

"The corporate environment in which we compete today is more focused on performance than ever, with an emphasis on profitable, sustainable growth. Translate that to mean maximizing total shareholder return, ruthless cost control, more accountability, return on investment, fact-based analysis, and transparency about everything we do. CEOs want the delivery of promises. They don't like surprises. They want a higher degree of discipline, analytical rigor, and a consistent and reasonable expectation of return for the investment that they are making in this important part of their balance sheet and P&L statement.

The fact is far too little has changed in the world of marketing and its perception, since Lord Leverhulme's famous quote: 'Half of what I spend is wasted. The trouble is I just don't know which half.' Some 70 years later, this is all too often how the marketing function is seen. Less than 50% effective, with serious, often high-profile doubts about which half is the effective half. We really do still have a long way to go.

So if marketing and brand building is to become a core part of the corporate DNA, to live up to the challenge we need to effect a dramatic shift. Essentially, we need to move the dial from 50% to 100% marketing effectiveness. How? We should take our cues from situation analysis and return to our internal competitor, in this case the finance function. Finance has three things going for it:

1. *People know what finance does for the company.*
2. *People believe they do it professionally and with rigor.*
3. *Most can prove their contribution absolutely, or at least they can prove it empirically.*

While there may be some doubt about the proof (we all know that even numbers can be deceptive and at odds with reality), numbers tend to be trusted implicitly. Disraeli first said, 'Lies, damn lies and statistics,' but that hasn't stopped the statisticians from influencing the CEOs and CFOs.

In contrast, what does marketing offer today? Too often, I believe, there is a lack of clear understanding of our role, a feeling that is often magnified in either financially oriented or sales-oriented companies. A slightly dilettante image: Is it really a profession like law or accounting or something else that we don't really comprehend? And truth be told, we have an unimpressive record of proving a solid return on investment.

What is our functional game plan to address this issue once and for all? Here are three core suggestions for your consideration:

■ *First and foremost, it is critical to get corporate understanding and more importantly buy-in of what marketing contributes to the good of the enterprise. No more hiding behind the veil of our own language and award shows.*

■ *Second, we need to build true professionalism throughout the function everywhere it operates.*

■ *And third, we need to establish clear accountability and measurement of the contribution that we are making.*

My experience with metrics and measurement is to make it simple if you want any chance of getting it done. Make it complex and it won't happen. At Diageo we have invested in a few very simple tools for our marketing investments with a bit of rigor behind them. The first we call the 'Dogs and Stars Chart'. It is a simple two-by-two matrix with the ROI on the vertical axis and the effect on the consumer (or brand-building power) on the horizontal. We plot all our activities.

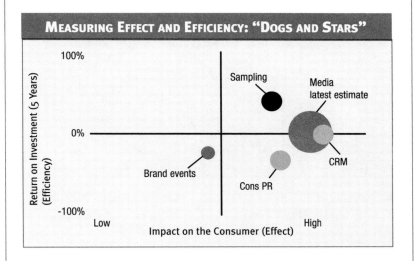

Things in the lower right-hand corner that are working with the consumer but not providing a return get our attention for how we might do them more efficiently. For those delivering great return on investment but not brand building, we look at how we might create a more sustainable effect on the consumer. Those in the bottom left-hand corner we don't do again. It is a very simple visual tool that marketers understand and buy into and finance directors love.

The second is a tracking chart that I review with our executive committee once a quarter. It is an analysis of the effectiveness of our advertising by brand, by medium, and by market for our top brands worldwide. When I first shared this chart, I was a bit nervous as it put on the line for all to see one of the most closely guarded marketing secrets — does our advertising really work? Does it really grow the business? The dark blue boxes are where the advertising has been running for more than a year and proving itself in business results and equity measures. The gray boxes are less than a year, but all the testing and equity measures are positive. The light blue boxes represent 'We don't know,' and the black boxes indicate 'We have a problem, we know it doesn't work, and we are working hard to solve it.' The arrows up or down indicate the change from the last quarter.

	BRAND X			BRAND Y			BRAND Z		
	TV	PRINT	O/D	TV	PRINT	O/D	TV	PRINT	O/D
GB	—				▼				
NA			▲						
Ireland									
Spain									
France			▲		new	new			
Portugal									
Greece									
Australia									
South Africa									
Mexico		▼							
Thailand						▲			

■ Proven Effective	■ Not Yet Proven	◆ Improvement	new Activity Added
■ Judged Effective	■ Unsatisfactory	◆ Decline	— Activity Discontinued

I knew we were on our way to building trust by the reaction of the CEO when I first put two imperfect scorecards that looked like this on the table and he said, 'This is the most honest and transparent presentation I have ever seen for marketing and I really do trust that you are on track to making the progress we need.' That is the start of the journey for the kind of professionalism and trust that we need to build for this function."[5]

CONCLUSION

At the outset of this book, we laid out several key benefits associated with the development and implementation of marketing dashboards. Specifically, we covered benefits related to:

- clarifying and defining the role of marketing in the company in a simple, transparent way that can be absorbed by different audiences quickly;

- reducing marketing jargon in favor of simple business terminology more likely to be understood in the boardroom, by the executive committee, and across the company;

- creating a learning organization that operates from a delivery system of facts and outcomes;

- eliminating functional silos within the marketing department that duplicate effort and foster unproductive competition for limited funding;

- discovering new measurement systems that fuel new ideas;

- establishing clearer roles and responsibilities within marketing organizations that lead to greater job satisfaction and a culture of performance and success; and

- putting marketing on a level playing field with other departments that can prove results and win valuable support and funding.

But all that is really just the logical rationalization for having a marketing dashboard.

The irreversible trend we've seen accelerating over the past 10 years in measurement of marketing effectiveness has dramatically improved both the return on marketing expenditures and the credibility of the marketing function within the corporation. Database technology, analytics, and Web presentation tools have all contributed to an unstoppable wave of desire to understand and quantify the impact of marketing expenditures on the company's bottom line. All this is unquestionably for the better.

But there is a much, much bigger game being played out in corporate boardrooms around the world, one in which dashboards are performing a critically important function. And sometimes marketers get so wrapped up in the financial and statistical orgy of metrics that we lose sight of the true competitive advantage afforded by an effective marketing dashboard.

The things that are countable can be counted by anyone. Given similar resources, competitors will always achieve parity with respect to the foundational elements of statistical analysis and optimization. Everyone will soon have their own media-mix model, and portfolio management of ROI will become the de facto standard for how marketing resources are allocated.

But what can truly separate us from our competitors and deliver exploitable marketplace advantage is not being better counters, but becoming better guessers.

Guessing is what we do when we don't have enough information to be certain about the likely outcome of a decision — which is most of the time.

There's a strange correlation between the potential magnitude of the risk of a given decision and the propensity to have to guess. The two are directly proportional. That's why people still manage companies and computers just provide "decision support."

An effective marketing dashboard facilitates becoming a better guessing organization in two ways:

1. It assembles the relevant information in a form and manner that improves the ability of the human mind to find the synaptic links between previously unrelated elements and see patterns where no numerical analysis has.
2. It provides a "learning loop" to rapidly test assumptions (a.k.a. "guesses") against observable facts to enhance the quality of the decisions in the face of uncertainty.

In a world of rapid assimilation of information, it's the development of proprietary insights that will distinguish one company from another. Insights can start out as just "guesses" but, through tools like the marketing dashboard, rapidly evolve to become known facts long before the competitors ever figure it out.

There's a famous picture of Albert Einstein sitting in his office in Princeton, NJ. On the wall above his shoulder, past his Mona Lisa smile, is a small plaque that reads:

> *Not everything that can be counted counts, and not everything that counts can be counted.*

Taken as a metaphor for marketing dashboard design and implementation, I think this is a very good framework for beginning or pursuing your journey of success.

SOURCES

1. *MarketingNPV Journal*, vol. 2, issue 1.

2. Malone, Thomas W., *The Future of Work: How the New Order of Business Will Shape Your Organization, Your Management Style, and Your Life*, Harvard Business School Press, 2004.

3. Light, Larry, McDonald's Corporation.

4. Ambler, Tim, *Marketing and The Bottom Line — 2nd Edition*, Financial Times Prentice Hall, 2003.

5. *MarketingNPV Journal*, vol. 1, issue 2.

Bibliography

Ambler, Tim, *Marketing and The Bottom Line — 2nd Edition*, Financial Times Prentice Hall, 2003.

Bacon, Lynd, "Graphical Data Analysis and Visualization Techniques for Marketing Research," AMA Art Forum Proceedings, 1996.

Few, Stephen, *Show Me the Numbers: Designing Tables and Graphs to Enlighten*, Analytics Press, 2004.

Kaplan, Robert S. & Norton, David P., *Strategy Maps: Converting Intangible Assets into Tangible Outcomes*, Harvard Business School Press, 2004.

Koller, Glenn, *Risk Assessment and Decision Making in Business and Industry, A Practical Guide — 2nd Edition*, Chapman & Hall/CRC, 2005.

Kosslyn, S.M., "Graphics and Human Information Processing," *Journal of the American Statistical Association*, 1985.

Lilien, Gary L. & Rangaswamy, Arvind, *Marketing Engineering: Computer Assisted Marketing Analysis and Planning*, Second Edition, Traford Publishing, 2004.

Malone, Thomas W., *The Future of Work: How the New Order of Business Will Shape Your Organization, Your Management Style, and Your Life*, Harvard Business School Press, 2004.

Schultz, Don & Schultz, Heidi, *IMC — The Next Generation: Five Steps for Delivering Value and Measuring Financial Return*, McGraw-Hill, 2003.

Shaw, Robert, *Improving Marketing Effectiveness: The Methods and Tools That Work Best*, Profile Books Ltd., 2000.

Index

Pat LaPointe

About the Author

Pat LaPointe is the Managing Partner at MarketingNPV. Pat directs the development of client solutions for CMOs in the areas of marketing measurement processes, tools, and skills to determine the financial return from marketing investments. His book *Marketing by the Dashboard Light: How to Get More Insight, Foresight, and Accountability from Your Marketing Investments* is a pioneering work on the topic of marketing dashboard development.

Pat's 20-year-plus career includes consulting with over half of the *Fortune* 100 and running large sales and marketing departments. His education credentials include an MBA from Stern School of Business at New York University and a Bachelor of Commerce from McGill University (Montreal).

About MarketingNPV

MarketingNPV is a highly specialized advisory firm that links marketing investments to financial value creation, enabling clients to measure the payback on their marketing efforts and take smarter risks with resource allocation. The firm provides processes and tools to identify and track the right performance metrics, and to anticipate the economic impact of possible changes in strategy or tactics. MarketingNPV maintains the world's largest online archive of articles and resources about marketing measurement, and publishes *MarketingNPV Journal* quarterly. For more information, visit **www.MarketingNPV.com**.